STRUGGLE & SURRENDER

A Roadmap Through the Wilderness

STRUGGLE & SURRENDER

A Roadmap Through the Wilderness

by G. Tyler Warner

Calvary Chapel Trussville
5239 Old Springville Rd, Pinson, AL, 35126
CalvaryChapelTrussville.com | Office@CalvaryChapelTrussville.com

STRUGGLE & SURRENDER
by G. Tyler Warner

© 2021 G. Tyler Warner
Published by Calvary Chapel of Trussville

5239 Old Springville Rd, Pinson, AL, 35126
CalvaryChapelTrussville.com
Office@CalvaryChapelTrussville.com

ISBN: 978-0-578-33076-1

For Catlyn, Zack, Sarah, Jacob, Ann, Zech and Emily

Thanks for following me into the wilderness.

1 Samuel 14:7

CONTENTS

Introduction 11

You Exist on Purpose: *The Birth of Jacob* 19

In the Middle of a Mess: *Jacob's Family History* 37

The Breaking Point: *Jacob's Deception* 57

Into the Wilderness: *The Flight of Jacob* 75

If God May Be Known: *Jacob's Dream at Bethel* 93

The Monster in the Mirror: *Jacob Meets Laban* 113

Fight the Right Way: *Laban Versus Jacob* 133

I Can't Take It Anymore! *Jacob Renounces Laban* 153

You've Got to Go Back: *Jacob Returns Home* 171

Death Before Life: *Jacob Wrestles with God* 189

A New Name: *Jacob Becomes Israel* 207

The Rest Is Up to You: *Jacob is Reunited with Esau* 225

Conclusion 243

INTRODUCTION

THE ROAD TO PERSONAL TRANSFORMATION

MY WILDERNESS

I was sitting in the truck on Exit 141 in Trussville. Traffic was bumper-to-bumper, right in the middle of rush hour. The back was overflowing with furniture, knick-knacks and old clothes, destined for the landfill first thing tomorrow. I had already been to various transfer stations five or six times that day. My blue uniform was filthy. It stank. So did the truck, and so did I, for that matter. The sun was beating down as I sat there feeling sorry for myself.

It had been more than a year since I left Virginia with my family to start the church in Alabama. Things were going alright, but progress seemed to have stalled. Attendance was growing, but just barely. We were still stuck meeting in the ballroom of the Hilton-Garden Inn. Not the big one, by the way, the little one. And as I sat there, my back hurting, my neck sweating, and the traffic boxing in all around me, I had a real moment of despair.

I had left behind a good job, most of my family, and some great prospects to plant this little church. I knew God had sent me, so I wasn't about to quit. But I had a few questions about His methods. I was tempted to believe that God had been spiteful by ripping me out of a promising trajectory and dropping me into painful obscurity.

I was in the wilderness.

We've all been there before. Times of questions, of testing, training and pain. I thought I was doing the right thing, but at what cost? I worried to my wife, "I've given up my whole life to come here." And then it clicked. That's exactly what I had done. But that was okay.

Jesus said in Luke 9:24,

"Whoever would save his life will lose it, but whoever loses his life for my sake will find it."

I was losing my life for Christ's sake. I had heard sermons on this verse my whole life, and had vowed that when my time came I wouldn't hesitate. This was my time! Once I realized that, the decision was easy. I wasn't going to give up, and I was going to stop feeling bad about it. In that moment, I crossed the river and left the wilderness. I still had months of work on the junk truck left, and there would be plenty of hurdles after that. But in my mind, this was the climax, the turning point. I had allowed God to break me, and I hadn't shamed myself by trying to go back to Egypt, so to speak. I had changed. I had grown and matured. I had undergone a very real personal transformation by the hand of the Holy Spirit.

THE EXAMPLE OF JACOB

The idea for this book came as I was teaching through Genesis at our church, Calvary Chapel Trussville. I began to consider turning the lessons on Jacob into a book even as I preached them. This story captivated me for a number of reasons.

First of all, it's just a good story. It's got vibrant characters, moments of danger and victory, and a narrative that feels cohesive.

Second, it's relatable. The Bible doesn't paper over its heroes' flaws. It focuses on them and uses them as examples to instruct us. I could see myself in Jacob, and that drew me to his story.

Third, it represents one of the clearest examples of the Bible's template of transformation. As you'll see, there is a distinctive track that Jacob follows, which is echoed in the lives of countless other heroes of the faith. For these reasons, I decided to focus on his life as a model for personal transformation.

WHAT THIS BOOK IS NOT

Notice that I said, "personal transformation," not, "self-transformation". I don't believe we can transform ourselves. So while this book has a lot in common with other self-help or motivational texts, it is distinctive in important ways.

This is a theological book. I have tried to make it approachable for the novice Christian and the curious unbeliever, but I am not ashamed to present the truth about God in a discussion about personal issues. The Bible does not just give us revelations about the end of time or the oddities of Heaven. It is a practical, everyday kind of Book, and I hope this little volume represents that well.

WHAT THIS BOOK IS

This book, as I mentioned, follows the biblical template for personal transformation. "Personal" because it has to do with us as individuals, although the Bible applies it to nations and even humanity as a whole. And "transformation" because that is exactly what we need. People don't need new rules or information, we need to be transformed from the inside out (Romans 12:1-2).

Through these chapters, we will walk with Jacob on his road to transformation. Each chapter will explain the relevant passage of Scripture, and then the broader theological principles. Good ideas lose credibility when we do not appropriately substantiate them from the Bible. Then each chapter will have a very practical section that applies the principle to your life. Then each chapter examines other examples from Scripture. This will give you a flavor for the fullness of these topics, although our primary focus will be Jacob.

HOW TO USE THIS BOOK

There are a number of ways you could read this book. It could be for information itself. You may not need to walk through this process, but it would still be good to familiarize yourself with it. There will be plenty of interesting lessons to learn along the way. You might read this book in order to help someone you love, maybe as a pastor or counselor. Nothing in here is so complicated that it could not be taught by someone else.

My vision for this book, though, is to provide a roadmap through the wilderness. It is something to be picked up when you are facing a crisis, and you are thrust out into the unknown. I promise not to give you my own theories and opinions, but to lead you straight to the source of wisdom that is the Word of God. I also see this book being used proactively to stave off a crisis; to handle a bad habit or a besetting sin that is going to cause trouble if not handled quickly.

That makes it all sound very serious, and it is that. But I have also tried to make it fun. There are plenty of stories and illustrations, and not a few pop-culture references. You may not be familiar with all of these, and that is fine. They are only illustrations, not endorsements or recommendations. I hope I've been able to draw out some worthy examples to aid in understanding the main points.

I have also recorded some short introductory videos for each chapter. If you're using this book in a small group or class, these will be very helpful. You can find these on CalvaryChapelTrussville.com or by visiting our YouTube channel

MY PRAYER FOR YOU

I don't mind admitting it. My prayer is that someone will find forgiveness in Jesus Christ through this book. I hope you don't see that as underhanded. I truly believe that the Gospel is the answer for every life and for all of life's troubles. That is a sweeping statement, but I make it very carefully. If you follow it through to the end, this book will lead you on a path to the ultimate personal transformation, that of salvation.

The rise in popularity of motivational books and online seminars and figures like Jordan Peterson or Deepak Chopra tells me that people are looking for answers. They are looking for direction and purpose in their life. I have great respect for that desire. I also have the answer. It is to be found in the book of books, the Bible itself. At the very least, we can admit that the wisdom of Genesis is greater than our own. We just might learn something if we deign to take it seriously.

15

But be warned! Taking the Bible seriously is a recipe for disaster as far as your self-life is concerned:

> "For the word of God is living and active, sharper than any two-edged sword, piercing to the division of soul and of spirit, of joints and of marrow, and discerning the thoughts and intents of the heart." (Hebrews 4:12)

The Bible will lay you open and expose who you really are. You may not like what you see.

But there is Good News. God is ready to change your life. He wants to use you to change the world around you. So let's take this journey with Jacob, whether for the first time or the hundredth time. May we be led by the Spirit thereby into deeper truth and greater transformation.

STUDY QUESTIONS

1.) What experience do you have with motivational or self-help books? How might a book coming from a Christian perspective be different?

2.) Have you read the story of Jacob before? What stands out to you from his story? How do you think the life of Jacob could be instructive for someone living in this day and age?

3.) How is personal transformation different from self-transformation? Do you agree that we cannot transform ourselves? Where do you think you might need transformation?

4.) Why are you reading this book? Are you in need of a change? Could any areas of your life benefit from a study like this one?

5.) Read Hebrews 4:12 again. How do you react to this description of the Bible? What kind of attitude towards the Bible should we have if this description is true?

1

YOU EXIST ON PURPOSE

THE BIRTH OF JACOB

(Genesis 25:19-23)

WHO IS SPECIAL?

I was born in 1991, which makes me a card-carrying Millennial. It also means I was brought up smothered by the infamous, "everyone gets a trophy", "everyone's a winner" mantra. Kids my age were raised by Saturday morning cartoons and enrichment programs to believe that we were all special, that being nice was the highest good, and that the only limit to our achievement was our own imagination.

Ironically enough, that saccharine message was delivered right alongside a different set of lessons. These were taught with equal authority and yet run exactly counter to the first. We were taught that the universe came into existence when an infinitely small ball of nothing exploded. Then the mud slowly but surely evolved into a little squishy thing that could eat and reproduce. After a lot of eating and reproducing, that thing turned into another thing, and the process continued until today. Now we, slightly more sophisticated squishy things, exist only to continue the process of consumption and reproduction.

Of course, it was never laid out that way. It was packaged as a kind of cosmic miracle, one that we were lucky to be a part of. But kids are smart, and over time they start to put two and two together. If we are adrift in an indifferent universe, a speck on a speck, with no future other than death, are we really so special?

There's a certain horror that comes on the heels of accepting such an idea. If nothing matters, then what is life, anyway? You can't think about that too long, you'll make yourself crazy. As the wildly popular *Rick and Morty* would say: "Nobody exists on purpose. Nobody belongs anywhere. Everybody's gonna die. Come watch TV."

"Nobody exists on purpose". That is the sad, cynical lesson that has taken root in the hearts of countless men and women, who are now struggling to find meaning in a world they have been convinced has none.

But remember, I am a 90's kid. I also grew up in church, and that combination means I've seen more *Veggie Tales* than you could calculate. At the end of every episode, I would hear the words, "Remember, God made you special, and He loves you very much!" Isn't that just the same sugary message that we heard everywhere else? It is not. There is one crucial component that the rest of the world misses: "God made you". You can tell people they're special all you want, but if you also tell them that they are just sentient stardust, the message won't stick. But if Morty is wrong, and we do exist on purpose – well, that changes everything.

We're going to follow the life of Jacob from start to finish. In fact, we're going to begin before the beginning. Because God had a plan for Jacob before he was even born. And God has a plan for you too. You exist on purpose. Maybe you've never heard that before. Maybe you've heard it and forgotten it, but it's true. There is a God. He knows about you, and He has a purpose for you.

I'm not going to take the time to prove this to you scientifically. The simple fact that believing in God is enough to transform the lives of terrorists, spousal abusers and murderers the world over is all the proof I need. And I think that your heart echoes with the truth of that statement.

You do matter. There is meaning to your life. And you exist on purpose.

CONTENDING IN THE WOMB

Genesis 25:19 is the beginning of a new subdivision in the first book of the Bible. Up till now we have seen the story of Abraham and his long wait for a promised son. That son was Isaac, the child of laughter. Isaac married Rebekah, the sister of Laban the Aramean (more on him later), and she too had trouble conceiving. Isaac was 40 years old when they were married, and 60 when the children were born. That means Isaac and Rebekah had twenty years of barrenness, waiting for their own promised child.

God answered Isaac's prayer, and Rebekah conceived. But in verse 22, it says, "The children struggled together within her". Rebekah was to have twins, but she had no way to know this. Apparently the two

21

boys were a handful even before birth! She went to the Lord for help, and He answered her with a remarkable prophecy:

> "The Lord said to her, 'Two nations are in your womb, and two peoples from within you shall be divided; the one shall be stronger than the other, the older shall serve the younger.'" (Genesis 25:23)

Not only was Rebekah carrying twins, she was given a glimpse of their futures. "Two nations," God called them, "two peoples". The twins in her womb would be named Jacob and Esau, and they would in fact grow to be fathers of mighty nations. So far this is nothing new. God had already promised both Abraham and Isaac that they would be the fathers of a multitude, of kings and nations (Genesis 15:5, 26:4). But what came next catches our eye.

He said, "the older shall serve the younger". The right of the firstborn was sacred in this culture, as it has been around the world. And the inheritance of Isaac was not just his land and property, but the Messianic Promise itself. God was messing with the usual order of things.

You might think that God knew Jacob would be more righteous than Esau, and so he deserved the blessing. But as we will see, that is a tough case to make. Jacob will indeed be more righteous than Esau, but it's difficult to say that his behavior is deserving of divine favor. So why is God making this announcement ahead of time?

The answer to that question is found in the New Testament, all the way over in the book of Romans. Paul explains,

> "When Rebekah had conceived children by one man, our forefather Isaac, though they were not yet born and had done

nothing either good or bad – in order that God's purpose of election might continue, not because of works but because of him who calls – she was told, 'The older will serve the younger.' As it is written, 'Jacob I loved, but Esau I hated.'" (Romans 9:10-13)

Paul deliberately draws out the innocence of the unborn babies here. Neither Esau nor Jacob had done anything that was "good or bad," so God's selection of Jacob was not based on merit or potential. Why then? He says, "In order that God's purpose of election might continue, not because of works, but because of him who calls." God chose the younger son instead of the older son because *He could.* God was asserting His sovereignty over the fulfillment of His Promise.

God had made a covenant with Abraham, choosing him to be the man through whom He would bless the world (Genesis 12:3). Abraham was to be the forefather of the One who would crush the head of the serpent and set the world to rights (Genesis 3:15). That blessing passed on to Isaac as Abraham's only trueborn son. The natural assumption is that the firstborn of Isaac would receive the blessing next.

But instead, God intervened. He chose the child no one would expect. God was reminding all of us that His blessing is not in the hands of men. It is not up to us to fulfill His promise, and nobody, by means of birth or anything else, can deserve His favor. The only thing that matters, as Paul explains, is "election," the calling and sovereign choice of God. That is why He "loved" Jacob and "hated" Esau (Malachi 1:2). It was not favoritism, but a free divine decision.

Clearly then, we can say that Jacob was born on purpose. There was a reason for his existence. He was conceived in answer to prayer, he was prophesied over before he was born, and God sovereignly chose him to be the one who would carry the Messianic hope. Election, purpose, destiny, intention. All these were Jacob's even before his little heart began to beat inside Rebekah's womb.

A PLAN AND A PURPOSE

How might it change your life to know that the same is true of you? I can hear the objections already: "Yes, Jacob was born on purpose, but he was a biblical hero! That kind of destiny is not for ordinary people like me." You think so? Let's see what God has to say.

The book of Psalms is a collection of songs. They are meant to be sung and prayed by all of God's people. These words are to be not just on the printed page, but in your mouth. And in Psalm 139, the Holy Spirit inspired the psalmist to give you this song:

"You formed my inward parts; you knitted me together in my mother's womb. I praise you, for I am fearfully and wonderfully made. Wonderful are your works; my soul knows it very well. My frame was not hidden from you, when I was being made in secret, intricately woven in the depths of the earth. Your eyes saw my unformed substance; in your book were written, every one of them, the days that were formed for me, when as yet there was none of them." (Psalm 139:13-16)

God handcrafted you in your mother's womb. Your days were planned out and established by God before you were a twinkle in anyone's eye but His. It doesn't matter how you were born, or what your parents might have told you. Repeat these words: "I am fearfully and wonderfully made." You are not an accident. You were created on purpose.

We were all born into the world, but the world is infected with sin. It's full of corruption; of nature, of society, of the body, of our very souls. Jacob will go on to be not only a victim of sin, but a perpetrator of its pain. So are we. That's why each one of us is in need of salvation. This book will be one long story of God saving Jacob from others and from himself. And the Good News is that God has sent His only Son Jesus to save the rest of us.

Paul famously wrote to the Ephesians,

"By grace you have been saved through faith. And this is not your own doing; it is the gift of God, not a result of works, so that no one may boast." (Ephesians 2:8-9)

When Jesus died on the cross, He became a substitute, a sacrifice to cover our sins. This is sure because of His Resurrection from the dead (Acts 17:31). Is this just a blanket blessing for the whole world? No, it's much better than that. Paul continues,

"For we are his workmanship, created in Christ Jesus for good works, which God prepared beforehand, that we should walk in them." (Ephesians 2:10)

God saved us so that we might fulfill the purpose for which He has created us. We are individually redeemed, not herded into Heaven like cattle. Jesus said,

"You did not choose me, but I chose you." (John 15:16)

Just as God handcrafted you in your mother's womb, Jesus handpicked you to be saved. Jacob was saved to fulfill his destiny as the father of Israel. And you too were saved on purpose.

Jacob had a calling on his life. He was announced as the heir of the Promise before his very birth. You have a calling on your life too.

> "Only let each person lead the life that the Lord has assigned to him, and to which God has called him." (1 Corinthians 7:17)

This verse tells us that "each person" has a life "assigned to him," that he has been "called" by God. A calling is an assignment from Heaven. It means you have a purpose that is unique to you as a subset of your calling to salvation. I'm not just talking about your career here, this is your whole life. There are works prepared for you to do. Just like Jacob, you were called on purpose.

As Jacob moves forward on his journey, he will encounter God, who will promise to be with him no matter what. He will promise to bless him and defeat his enemies. In effect, God promises to give him everything he needs in order to fulfill the calling on his life. You're ahead of me by now – the same is true of you.

On the day of Pentecost, the Holy Spirit rushed upon the Church for the first time (Acts 2). The book of Acts chronicles the partnership between the Church and the Holy Spirit to accomplish the mission of evangelism. And if you belong to Christ, then this promise is for you too (Acts 2:39). The Holy Spirit dwells within you, and He has something for you:

> "To each is given the manifestation of the Spirit for the common good." (1 Corinthians 12:7)

The Holy Spirit has specifically empowered you to fulfill your calling. Not only have you been handmade and handpicked and called, you have been uniquely gifted to live the life God has planned for you. Jacob is not the only one with divine help. You have been gifted, by God, on purpose.

This might be a surprise to you. And you still might not believe it, because you've never seen it. Jacob was prophesied over, and God appeared to him at Bethel. He was informed about his purpose while you feel like you're scrabbling in the dark. But God wants to shine a light on the meaning of your life.

Paul prayed for the church in Colossae,

"We have not ceased to pray for you, asking that you may be filled with the knowledge of his will in all spiritual wisdom and understanding." (Colossians 1:9)

Did you see that? "Knowledge" and "wisdom" and "understanding". We are directed by the example of the apostle to seek to know the will of God. God wants you to know His will for your life, He will not keep it a secret. He wants you to have the wisdom of how to do His will, and He wants you to understand it.

God is not coy with your calling. Jacob was given divine revelation about the purpose for his life, and God wants to do the same for you. He will see to it that you are informed, on purpose.

The Scriptures show us that we are not so different from the heroes we read about. The details of our lives may be different, but God treats us the same way. Your life is parallel to that of Jacob. Both of you were created on purpose, saved on purpose, called on purpose, gifted on purpose and informed on purpose. God does everything with intention and will. You are no accident. You are part of His plan, and He has done everything necessary to make it happen.

MINDSET SHIFT

I'm sure you detected the sarcasm earlier when I spoke about the "everybody's special" drumbeat of my childhood. You can see that same scorn in Pixar's film, *The Incredibles*: "Everyone's special, Dash," says Mrs. Incredible to her son. "Which is just another way of saying no one is," he replies glumly. Many kids raised like me have determined to be more realistic with their kids.

This is usually explained in terms of scale: You are just one out of millions of young athletes, the odds of you making it in the NFL are slim to none. Your country is just one among many, and everyone thinks theirs is the best. This planet is just one of several in a medium-sized solar system in a common galaxy in a universe so big it cannot even be comprehended. "I'm significant!" cried the boy from *Calvin & Hobbes*. He stared at the vastness of space for a moment, then whispered, "Screamed the dust speck".

Even in the Church, there are many who want to put a stop to all this talk of "calling". Oddly, this comes from the most conservative, orthodox corners. Plenty of ink is spilled denouncing books and ministries that focus on the individual's purpose (I suppose they'll have to add this one to the pile). If any talk is to be made about special calling, or unique purpose, it is to be applied to the Church as a whole: You are part of the chosen people, and you are not especially significant within that group!

But I think the clamor after these (sometimes aberrant) ministries reveals a legitimate hunger for God and His promised abundant life (John 10:10). The Gospel is certainly not just another how-to manual for success, but it does provide the spiritual answers to the questions of the multitudes. Even if, like James and John, they do not know exactly what they're asking for (Mark 10:38-39).

Before we can continue, you must believe that God has in fact made you special, and that He does have an individual plan for your individual life. Perhaps like the cynical scientists or the stuffy religious scolds, you wonder how that could be possible. You're not alone. Check this out from the book of Psalms:

"When I look at your heavens, the work of your fingers, the moon and the stars, which you have set in place, what is man that you are mindful of him, and the son of man that you care for him?" (Psalm 8:3-4)

Even in Scripture, the soul of man wonders how God could possibly care for him while the universe spins in all its vast grandeur around him. But the important difference is what frames the wonder of the psalmist:

"Yet you have made him a little lower than the heavenly beings and crowned him with glory and honor. You have given him dominion over all the works of your hands; you have put all things under his feet." (Psalm 8:5-6)

We see the bigness of the world and conclude that we don't matter. The Bible sees the bigness of the world and affirms that we do matter, and then tries to understand how both can be true. Why? Because God has told us, in no uncertain terms, that He loves us and cares for us individually, and that there is a purpose and plan for each one of us.

How does that change your life? The way the hero of every story's life is changed when he realizes he is not just a farm boy or lost orphan, but is destined for great things. I hope you can feel the sun rising in your heart already.

There should be great joy! In Acts 3, when Peter and John healed a lame man at the gate of the Temple, it says he "entered the temple with them, walking and leaping and praising God" (Acts 3:8). The fruit of the Spirit is joy unspeakable (Galatians 5:22, 1 Peter 1:8). When your life is touched by Jesus, a celebration enters your heart that no sorrow can touch. Despite all your failures, God has redeemed you to fulfill the purpose of your life. The despair of the 21st Century has met its match in the grace of Almighty God. How about a smile?

Also, it should produce a sense of responsibility. The other deficiency of our time is that of purpose. But if we are loved and chosen by God, what better reason is there to get out of bed in the morning? When you realize that Christ has saved you, not just to be another notch on His Bible, but for a real purpose, it should fill you up with motivation to accomplish that purpose.

It's time to shift your mindset. You are wonderfully made and specifically chosen by God. Rejoice in those truths! And then get to work about the business to which He has called you. Let's leave behind the scoffing of a hopeless world and the clucking of ice-cold Christians. It is the ones who are set on fire who will accomplish the Mission.

GOD'S CHOSEN ONES

Is it hard for you to accept that you exist on purpose, and that you have a God-given destiny? You're not alone. Just look at what God said to Jeremiah:

"Before I formed you in the womb I knew you, and before you were born I consecrated you; I appointed you a prophet to the nations." (Jeremiah 1:5)

This is what we're talking about: that foreknowledge, that wonderful predestination! It's a lot to take in. At least it was for Jeremiah:

"Then I said, 'Ah, Lord God! Behold, I do not know how to speak, for I am only a youth.'" (Jeremiah 1:6)

Jeremiah was sure God had the wrong guy. He was too young, too untrained. Moses had similar complaints: too old, bad reputation, speech impediment, God, you'd better find somebody else (Exodus 4). What's your excuse? Lay it out there, God's not afraid to hear it. But don't expect Him to let you off easy.

"But the Lord said to me, 'Do not say, 'I am only a youth" for to all to whom I send you, you shall go, and whatever I command you, you shall speak." (Jeremiah 1:7)

God did not want to hear Jeremiah's excuses. Nor Moses's ("Who has made man's mouth?"). And right now, He is kindly and patiently telling you that your excuses are not acceptable.

You might wonder how you could ever live up to such a destiny. For some, it is easier to crawl into a hole and be nobody than to shoot for the moon and miss. But God promised to be with Moses and Jeremiah, and He'll be with you, too.

"Do not be afraid of them, for I am with you to deliver you, declares the Lord." (Jeremiah 1:8)

Many biblical heroes and saints of Church History were reluctant at first. I think of Saul, who hid among the baggage at his own coronation (1 Samuel 10:22). Gideon made God prove his calling over and over again before he believed (Judges 6).

Others rush in, excited at the prospect of a God-given purpose, only to have that crisis of faith later. Moses was one of these (Acts 7:25). Elijah prayed for death after calling down fire from Heaven (1 Kings 19:4). John the Baptist doubted Jesus from prison (Matthew 11:2-3), and Peter denied Him three times (Luke 22:61).

What will carry us through these moments is the absolute surety that God has called us by name and sent us out about His business. I am sure that Samuel leaned heavily on the first time he heard God's voice call him in the Tabernacle (1 Samuel 3). In the wilderness, David wrote songs about relying on God's promises to him (Psalm 57). Paul told the story of his Damascus road conversion to anyone who would listen (Acts 26).

So too, you must stand beside your brothers and sisters who have gone before you. Plant these truths deep in your heart so they can grow unshakeable roots. We cannot skip to the practical stuff. You must believe that you exist on purpose. Not because of any scientific proof or miraculous demonstration, but because God said so in His Word.

"The Lord your God is in your midst, a mighty one who will save; he will rejoice over you with gladness; he will quiet you by his love; he will exult over you with loud singing." (Zephaniah 3:17)

FRESH PERSPECTIVE

There are those who think that belief in God, and thereby objective purpose in life, is a fairy story for dumb people. Some folks believe they are just too smart to be saved. These are constantly trying to hammer home the bleak reality of their worldview. I've even heard it said that to teach your children to believe in God is child abuse. I find that utterly risible. Is it abusive to tell children repeatedly: "God made you special, and He loves you very much"?

How smart is being smart if it guts all the best parts of life? I don't see pessimism and cynicism as the marks of high intellect. Jesus told us to judge teachings and teachers by the fruit they produce (Matthew 7:20). If belief in nothing but the cold loneliness of space leads to that kind of existential horror, then perhaps it is better to reject it out of hand. I refuse to bow to a philosophy that has no room for beauty or valor or meaning. You must insist upon an explanation that can account for the great intangibles of life.

The Gospel is exactly that explanation. God made the world. He made you. He has a plan and a purpose for you. He sent His Son Jesus to save you, and He sent His Holy Spirit to help you fulfill your mission. You have a destiny, a future, and a hope that will never disappoint. Like Jacob, you have a path to tread for the glory of God and the good of your own soul. Take hold of that and stand on it in unwavering faith.

You are not an accident; you exist on purpose.

And God loves you very much.

STUDY QUESTIONS

1.) Have you had any experience with the "everybody's special" message? How about evolution and cosmic insignificance? Do you see them positively or negatively?

2.) Can you understand the cynicism that comes from the combination of these lessons? Where in society or pop culture have you seen this angst expressed? How about in your own life?

3.) How does the prophecy of Jacob's birth set the stage for his life? How does Paul's analysis in Romans 9:10-13 affect the way we read this story?

4.) Is it hard for you to think of yourself in the same category as biblical heroes like Jacob? Why?

5.) How does it make you feel to know that you have been created with a plan and a purpose? Is it hard for you to accept that? Is it reassuring to read the Scriptures that prove it?

6.) Why do you think so many people are attracted to teachers that talk about calling and meaning? Why do others disapprove of such teachers? Is there a balance to be struck?

7.) Why does the knowledge of your calling produce joy? Why does it produce responsibility? Have you felt these things yourself?

8.) If believing there is no purpose in life leads to depression and heartache, what might that say about the truth of that belief? How about the fact that believing in God's calling leads to joy and responsibility?

9.) Can you relate to Jeremiah's protests when God called him? How about Moses? What did God have to say to them when they objected? What might God say to you?

10.) Do you know what your calling is? If not, what steps could you take to find out? If so, what steps are you taking to fulfill it?

2

IN THE MIDDLE OF
A MESS

JACOB'S FAMILY HISTORY

(Genesis 25:24-34)

THE PRESSURE OF POTENTIAL

The joy of being young is its boundless potential. Especially if you are reasonably sociable and talented, the world feels like an exciting adventure just waiting to happen. And it is! God has created each one of us with a plan and a purpose. There are few ideas more exciting than that.

But as you get older, potential becomes less and less of an asset. It's okay to be skilled but undisciplined when you're 16. It's less acceptable when you're 36. And as time goes on, you start to hear that word, "wasted", put in front of your potential.

This is an intimidating prospect. You may have it in you to do something incredible, but for that to mean anything, it's got to come out. "Well," we say, "I won't think about that now, there's plenty of time!" But graduations, birthdays and anniversaries remind us that the clock is ticking. Sooner or later, we're going to have to do something with all that potential.

You can ignore it, and ride through life as if on rails: taking jobs, getting married, spending money, with no intention behind it. That's a recipe for bitterness, right there. You can overthink it and freeze up; staying in the same places, wearing the same clothes and working the same kind of job out of fear that you'll mess up. That's a recipe for serious anxiety and despair. Or you can refuse to believe it and do nothing; insist that eventually things will come around, regardless of effort on your part. And that is a recipe for rage. Rage against your family, your boss, the "system", even God.

None of these responses are righteous. Wasting your life is not just self-destructive, but causes a ton of collateral damage. Even little things like bad habits or unrestrained character flaws have a ripple effect on the whole world.

If God has created you for a purpose, what does it mean if you refuse to live it out? It means that God's wonderful ideal will never be realized. Your family, your community, your church, will all have to settle for less than what God intended – because of you. We need what you have to give.

It may terrify you to think that God has high expectations of you. And as you look around at your relationships, your spiritual life, even the state of your room, you might see very little prospect of God's wonderful pronouncements ever coming true. The "now" of your life bears little resemblance to the glorious future He has planned for you.

But there is another way. Rather than ignoring it or panicking, you can be honest with yourself and get to work. Have you ever been afraid to check your bank statement because you know you might be overdrawn? Failing to look solves nothing. It's the same thing with your life. You must be willing to examine your behavior, your marriage, or even your nation and assess it with sobriety. Honest self-evaluation is the first step toward the life God has laid out before you.

You are essential to the edification of the Church and the expansion of the Kingdom. God has no throwaway people. You're not ready yet, but He wants to make you ready. He loves you just as you are, but He loves you too much to leave you that way. That's why you must take stock of the way things are right now and face them squarely. Or you will never get there. There's no mulligans, no restarts, there's just you.

"Search me, O God," David prayed, "and know my heart! Try me and know my thoughts!" (Psalm 139:23) If you want to move forward with your life, as Keith Green sang, "You've got to start right here".

REAL LIFE IS MESSY

Isaac was the child of laughter, the promised son of Abraham himself. And with the birth of the twins, the fragile line of promise was secure for another generation. Surely this family, as significant as they were in the story of salvation history, would stand apart from the rest of men. At least, that's how the Bible would try to spin their story, right?

Not exactly.

Rebekah gave birth to twin boys, fulfilling the word of the Lord. Right away, we can see that the differences between these two were going to far outweigh the similarities.

"The first came out red, all his body like a hairy cloak, so they called his name Esau." (Genesis 25:25)

The elder twin is so hairy they decide to name him exactly that – *Esau* means "hairy". This is going to be a major plot point later, so it's important that you grasp this: Esau was a hairy dude! It reminds me of that line Gaston sings in *Beauty & the Beast*. And actually, that character is pretty close to what we know of Esau from this chapter.

"When the boys grew up, Esau was a skillful hunter, a man of the field." (Genesis 25:27)

Esau was a man's man. He didn't want to stay inside, he wanted to be out in the wilderness, testing his mettle against the elements. He was a hunter and an outdoorsman. He shopped at Bass Pro Shops. He wore a hat with a fishhook on it, and a flannel shirt with the sleeves cut off. He drove a lifted truck with a shotgun hanging in the window. A few deer carcasses in the back. Later on, Esau would take the nickname Edom, which means "red". So imagine, if you will, a loud, hairy redneck named Big Red. That's Esau.

Now, of course there's nothing wrong with being a tough guy. But in the Bible, there are a lot of negative connotations related to Esau's chosen activities. To be a "skilled hunter" reminds us of Nimrod from Genesis 10, a wicked warlord who founded such nations as Assyria and Babylon. The implication is that to be a "hunter" was to be a "hunter of men," that is, an assassin or raider. In this passage the only thing Esau hunts is a deer for its venison. But at the end of his life, we will find Esau living as a raider in the land of Seir, conquering nations:

40

a hunter of men. He was also a womanizer and a profane man with little interest in spiritual things (Hebrews 12:16).

This is when we would expect the Bible to introduce a counterpoint: an Abel for Cain, a David for Goliath. And in a way, that's what we get. But Esau's brother is not quite what you'd expect. At their birth we read,

> "Afterward [Esau's] brother came out with his hand holding Esau's heel, so his name was called Jacob." (Genesis 25:26)

The younger twin was holding on to his brother's heel as they were born, as if he were trying to hold him back so he could be born first. That explains the distress Rebekah felt during her pregnancy! This gives us the meaning of Jacob's name, *Yacov*, which means "heel catcher". Imagine an Olympic sprinter reaching out to trip up the man in first place; that's a Heel-Catcher. It implies "trickster, cheater", or as Gayle Erwin likes to say: "Dirty, Sneaky Thief"!

Jacob turns out nothing like his brother.

"Jacob was a quiet man, dwelling in tents." (Genesis 25:27)

This is an interesting point of translation. The Hebrew for "quiet" is *tam*, which is usually translated "upright" or "whole". For this reason, some have tried to interpret Jacob's behavior as blameless and holy. But that becomes increasingly difficult as we read his story. In context, it is best to understand that word to mean "quiet", or "civilized", as explained by "dwelling in tents". It's a contrast to Esau, the wild man out in the woods.

Jacob was a rule-follower; we might say a goody two-shoes. He does not strike us as masculine or forceful. Jacob preferred to be clean and comfortable. He liked to cook and didn't mind helping out with the household chores. He wore skinny jeans and a scarf in summertime. His glasses had dark rims, and his hair hung down into his eyes just so. No nickname for him, he hated it when Esau called him "Jake". He was a quiet, introverted hipster. He didn't break the rules – not because he was such a good guy, but because he was soft and compliant, unwilling to make waves. And as many quiet, well-behaved men do, Jacob resorted to trickery and manipulation to get what he wanted He was just as aggressive as his brother, but his was a passive aggression. Unworthy qualities for a patriarch of the Promise!

So you've got Esau the wild child and Jacob the sneaky citizen. Depending on your demeanor, you probably identify with one or the other. That's what happened with their parents, too.

"Isaac loved Esau because he ate of his game, but Rebekah loved Jacob." (Genesis 25:28)

Dad, of course, loved that he had raised such a macho son. And those steaks weren't bad either. Isaac is something of a glutton and a hypochondriac in this story. On the other hand, Rebekah preferred the quiet, well-behaved boy, as most moms would. She was the sister of Laban, the consummate trickster, and it showed. She would teach her favorite son how to get his way through backdoor channels as she and Isaac played the boys off of one another.

There came a day when "Esau came in from the field, and he was exhausted". He saw Jacob cooking some red stew and asked for some.

"Jacob said, 'Sell me your birthright now.' Esau said, 'I am about to die; of what use is a birthright to me?'" And so, "he swore to him and sold his birthright to Jacob." (Genesis 25:29-34)

Here we see the twins at their worst. Esau chose a bowl of soup over the Promise that Abraham had sojourned for, and Jacob exploited his brother's recklessness to grab the birthright for himself.

What a mess. They were buying and selling the Messianic hope! You call this God's chosen family? Yes. This story, some version of which is being played out in countless suburbs around America, was also the story of God's great Promise. God had his eye on this family, and He had already chosen Jacob to carry on the Covenant. But Jacob was not ready yet. At this point he was a full-on contributor to his dysfunctional family. Which is exactly why God needed him. He would use him to lead these people out of their selfishness and shortsightedness.

The Bible does not soften its evaluation of the situation. It sets us an example of how we must look at ourselves and those we love. Yes, Jacob was in a difficult position, caught in the middle of his two parents, at odds with his spirited brother. But he had his own flaws too. Despite outward appearances, he was a conniving Heel-Catcher. This kind of assessment is not fun, it's not encouraging. But it is absolutely necessary. It's how God looks at us. And if we want to walk with God, we must be willing to look at things the way He does.

PROPHETIC ASSESSMENT

Throughout the Bible, God made use of men called prophets. In short, a prophet is someone who speaks for God. These were useful men to have around. The kings especially would keep prophets at court to inquire of the Lord before battle or other major decisions. But the prophets were also in a dangerous position. In times of rebellion and sin, the prophets only ever had bad news. One such prophet was imprisoned by the wicked King Ahab because, as the king said, "I hate him, for he never prophesies good concerning me, but evil" (1 Kings 22:8). We laugh, because what kind of prophet would he be if he only told the king what he wanted to hear? But we all fall into this trap. Paul warned us against finding "teachers to suit [our] own passions" (2 Timothy 4:3). God has no patience for people who refuse to hear the truth.

God is truth. Jesus Himself said, "I am...the truth" (John 14:6). The Holy Spirit is called "the Spirit of truth" (John 14:17). And everyone who would be a worshiper of God "must worship in spirit and truth" (John 4:24). God is not a fan of avoidance, and is certainly not a fan of lies, not even those pleasant little lies we tell ourselves to feel better about our mess. He sends His prophets to force people to face the truth of their sinful situations.

For example, that last reference to worship in "spirit and truth" comes from a story in the Gospel of John. Jesus encountered a woman who was running full speed away from the truth of her own life. She found Jesus at the well in Samaria and He asked her for water. She, a Samaritan, tried to pick a fight with Him, but Jesus patiently discussed her questions. Then He asked her to fetch her husband so He could talk to them both.

> "The woman answered him, 'I have no husband.' Jesus said to her, 'You are right in saying, 'I have no husband'; for you have had five husbands, and the one you now have is not your husband. What you have said is true.'" (John 4:17-18)

44

This woman was spunky and ready to discuss the deep questions, but had failed to acknowledge the mess she had made for herself. Jesus, the perfect Prophet, gently exposed her to the sad state of her own life. Clearly, she had issues with men. I'm sure there were a lot of bad decisions and terrible heartbreaks in her past. She was not prepared to deal with it. But when she met Jesus, she was forced to confront the reality of her life.

That is what we must do. It does us no good to go on whistling Dixie in the middle of a mess. Failing to admit your deteriorating health because of your gluttony is foolish. Refusing to think about your awful work situation solves nothing. Ignoring the growing distance between you and your children is downright dangerous. If you can't take a hard look at your life, you will never realize the destiny God has for you.

When the woman at the well was willing to face the truth of her life, God used her to establish the first foothold of the Kingdom of Heaven in Samaria.

> "The woman left her water jar and went away into town and said to the people, 'Come, see a man who told me all that I ever did. Can this be the Christ?'" (John 4:28-29)

What saved this woman was the honest assessment of her situation. It made her vulnerable enough to receive the living water of Jesus Christ.

You might think that you can avoid the growing rot, and still move on in your spiritual life. You are deceiving yourself. Eli the priest was the judge and spiritual leader of Israel. But Eli had a problem with his children. His two sons, Hophni and Phineas, were priests as well. Eli may have been a good man, but his boys were rotten to the core. "Worthless men," the Bible calls them. They used to steal the best portions of the sacrifices for themselves, and they used their position to sexually exploit the young women who served at the Tabernacle (1 Samuel 2:12-22). Eli gave them a stern talking-to, but he did nothing to put a stop to their actions (1 Samuel 3:13). When the young Samuel received his first prophetic vision, Eli was finally forced to hear what God thought of the situation (1 Samuel 3:18).

Ignoring problems only makes them worse. I used to work for a company that cleared out people's junk. I have been in many hoarders' houses. In many cases, the main part of the house looked fine, but there was a closed-off room or attic that was jam-packed to the top with junk – clothes, furniture, food, you name it. Although the house looked nice, it smelled horrible. The floors were rotting, there could be vermin, and nobody wanted to come around. The owners were so used to it, they hardly noticed. But you could see the shame on their faces when they were forced to open "that door" and confront what was inside. We all need the prophetic voice that forces us to open doors we would rather keep shut.

God expects us to evaluate our lives through His eyes. We cannot ignore the mess, and we cannot try to move past the mess without cleaning it up. It is very likely that your mess is exactly what God has called you to clean up first. And when you do, like the woman at the well, you will begin to see transformation. But if you refuse to see what is right in front of you – your personal vices, your family dysfunctions, your country's generational sins – there is only tragedy awaiting you, like Eli and his sons. Paul told the Corinthians, "Examine yourselves" (2 Corinthians 13:5). Have you done that?

LOOK IN THE MIRROR

Procrastination and avoidance are dream-killers. They must be disposed of immediately. Jacob was prophesied to carry the Promise for another generation, and become the father of Israel. No doubt he consoled himself with starry dreams of the day when he would be patriarch. But when we look at his family, and him in particular, it's clear that there was a long way to go. Daydreams don't solve problems.

What is the status of your own life right now? You might not know your calling, or maybe you do. But either way, you must begin that journey by taking stock of your life. That's what prophets were for, to insist that people look in the mirror. I'm willing to bet that you are very well aware of your situation, in all its embarrassing messiness. But don't convince yourself that it will all work itself out someday because you've got a destiny. You do, but that should only drive you to get started. Looking in the mirror and then failing to act on it is self-deception (James 1:22-25).

Start by looking at yourself: what is your character? Maybe you're like Esau. You're loud and wild and very pleased with yourself. But you have little appetite for spiritual things, and you hurt people around you with your thoughtlessness. Maybe you've lived long enough to see the murderous results of your unchecked rage, selfishness and violence.

Or maybe you're like Jacob. Everyone commends you as a good boy. You keep the rules outwardly, but inside you resent every minute of it. You hate those who are confident and capable, because you are not. You don't want to grow up and leave home, because you're scared. And everyone around you mistakes your fear for virtue. You're sneaky and passive-aggressive and manipulative; a Heel-Catcher. And given

47

the right opportunity, you would show yourself to be just as rotten as the Esaus in your life.

Look at your family. What issues are brewing between you? Where are the battle lines drawn, who is on whose team? Do you and your wife constantly test each other and punish one another when you're unhappy? Maybe the kids know just how to work mom and dad to get what they want. There could be drugs or alcohol involved, sexual or verbal abuse, obsession with money or accomplishment or work or school. Who rules the roost, and who broods in the corner? Many families have a relative who insists on having a finger in everybody's business. Is that you? What is your family's mess?

You could expand this out to your church. Churches can be hotbeds of gossip and political maneuvering. Consider your school or workplace. Are there fault lines in place just waiting for a big shakeup? It can be cheap and easy to evaluate the nation, but that's part of it too. We must take a hard look at where we are so we can get to where we're going. When Ernest Shackleton and the crew of the *Endurance* were stranded in Antarctica, the trouble was not knowing where they needed to go, but their inability to determine their location.

And don't just look at the big things. There was an episode of *The Dog Whisperer* when Cesar Milan was called to help a family with their big old mutt who was terrorizing their little lapdog. But as Cesar observed their interactions, it became clear that it was the yappy little one who was instigating the problems. Because the big dog's bark was so loud, the family assumed that he was the issue. So it is in your life. The obvious thing might not be the problem. Look very closely to determine where things are going wrong.

This can be a very hard thing. You love your family, and recognizing your issues, even major ones, can be heartbreaking. It might be less so for your job, until you realize how you yourself are contributing to the very thing you hate about it. And you might be all too familiar with your own shortcomings; but as painful as it might be, you've got to look. Don't numb yourself with another drink or hit or video game or scroll through Instagram. Take the time to get quiet, pray, and let the Lord reveal to you the reality of the current situation.

God wants to form you into the image of His Son, Jesus. But you can quench His Holy Spirit by your refusal to consider your ways. Have you found that every time you get serious about prayer, or reading your Bible, you come back to the same application point? Maybe verses about gossip keep popping up, or the preacher seems to always be talking about pornography. You need to sit up and listen, because God might be trying to tell you something.

So many of my generation have failed to take even this first simple step. They find themselves in a state of arrested development, unable to move out of their adolescence. It could be fear, it could be laziness, it could be any number of things. But until we can stop and admit our childish attitude, our obsession with trivial things, our inability to commit to a relationship, our out-of-control consumption of fast food, and our slothful refusal to keep to a normal schedule, nothing is going to change. And if we keep trying to bypass these practical matters and focus on so-called spiritual things, we will keep stalling out. Because dealing with these things is in fact real spiritual growth. It's time to face it.

You've got dreams. You've got aspirations. But if you're not willing to grow into the kind of person who can accomplish those dreams, they'll never happen. Is it going to take a prophet pushing you beyond your breaking point to get you to stare your insufficiency in the face?

Realizing who you really are might break your heart, but it will be worth it if it forces you to start moving forward.

I AM A SINFUL MAN

All great men of God have to go through this. Some men have little trouble making an honest appraisal of themselves. Others have to be nudged a little.

Let's look at Simon Peter. His calling was to be first among the apostles, one of the greatest evangelists of all time. He would write two epistles of the New Testament and his testimony would serve as the basis for Mark's Gospel. He would personally open the door to the Gentiles in the Church, and would eventually be crucified upside-down in Rome. "You are Peter," Jesus said, "and on this rock I will build my church" (Matthew 16:18).

But Peter had a problem (as did the other disciples) with pride. He always tended to evaluate himself too highly. And so Jesus graciously provided him with an opportunity to see who he really was. In Luke 5, Jesus preached out of Simon's boat while he mended his nets. After the sermon, in the heat of the day, Jesus asked to go fishing on the Sea of Galilee.

"And Simon answered, 'Master, we toiled all night and took nothing! But at your word I will let down the nets.'" (Luke 5:5)

Peter was exasperated with this tourist after a long night of fruitless fishing. But you know the story. They hauled in so many fish, two boats could not hold them all.

"But when Simon Peter saw it, he fell down at Jesus' knees, saying, 'Depart from me, for I am a sinful man, O Lord.'" (Luke 5:8)

Face to face with his own shortcomings, Simon knew he had no right to be in the presence of Jesus. He knew that he did not deserve the calling God had prepared for him. But Jesus made him His disciple, a fisher of men (Luke 5:10). When we are willing to be honest with ourselves and with God, we become usable in His hands.

Moses had a similar problem. He grew up in Pharaoh's house as something of a novelty – a Hebrew in the king's court. When he was grown, however, he began to take an interest in his people's plight. He murdered an Egyptian for beating a Hebrew because,

"He supposed that his brothers would understand that God was giving them salvation by his hand." (Acts 7:25)

Moses thought very highly of himself and very naively about the situation. The failure of the Hebrews to rise up and follow their would-be Spartacus drove him into the wilderness, where he spent forty years herding sheep. When God appeared to him in the burning bush, Moses had changed his tune.

"Who am I that I should go to Pharaoh and bring the children of Israel out of Egypt?" (Exodus 3:11)

Now he could see the seriousness of the problem, not as a pampered prince, but as an older, wiser man. And he could see himself for who he truly was: timid and not well-spoken. Actually, Moses thought too little of himself. He tried several times to get out of his calling, until "the anger of the Lord was kindled" (Exodus 4:14). He had learned humility, but it had turned to fear, which is never of the Lord. If you think so little of yourself that not even God can use you, then you also need a fresh look at your life.

Whether you are in the position of thinking too highly of yourself, like Peter or Moses, or thinking too little of yourself and not enough of God, like Gideon (Judges 6:15), it's time to reassess. Take a long, hard look at where you are now. In fact, take a picture, because you're not going to be here for long! Get your bearings so you can start moving forward. But get those bearings first, or you'll end up lost. Samson tried to work out God's calling for himself without looking to his own life, and it ended in tragedy. It wasn't until his eyes had been put out that he could truly see himself and his God for who they really were (Judges 16:28).

WHAT IS IN YOUR HAND?

I'm not trying to make you feel bad. But I am trying to get you to feel the fullness of what is going on around you. Such assessment can provoke feelings of sadness, rage, regret, even despair. These things must be known and felt deeply before we can begin. But it's not just making a list of everything that's wrong. It's an act of the spiritual imagination, as we consider what these things could be when God redeems them.

When Moses doubted God's call at the burning bush,

"The Lord said to him, 'What is that in your hand?' He said, 'A staff.'" (Exodus 4:2)

God did amazing things through Moses' simple staff. It was his shepherd's tool, a symbol of his shame, his exile and his failure. But with it, God would smite Egypt with plagues, part the Red Sea, and grant Israel victory over the Amalekites. So it is very important that you know what is "in your hand". Because God wants to do amazing things with it.

Consider the story of Tabitha. She was a Christian in Joppa in the first days of the Church. "She was full of good works and acts of charity" the Bible says (Acts 9:36). She sewed garments for the poor and the widows. Such a simple thing! But when she died, the church in Joppa was so distraught they called for Peter.

> "All the widows stood beside him weeping and showing tunics and other garments that [she] had made." (Acts 9:39)

Peter, alone with the body, prayed, and God raised Tabitha from the dead! The joy of the church was contagious.

> "It became known throughout all Joppa, and many believed in the Lord." (Acts 9:42)

You might think to yourself, "I want to serve God. I want people to be blessed by my life. I want to see miracles, I want to see revival in my city!" I'm sure Tabitha thought the same things. But all she had in her hand was a sewing needle. She couldn't preach like Peter, or do miracles like Philip. She just sewed. That could have been a discouragement to her. Her self-evaluation would not have impressed any of us. But she did not despair over what she did not have.

She just sewed.

And because Tabitha sewed, the church in Joppa was brought together as a community. Because she sewed, widows were comforted in their grief. Because she sewed, a mighty miracle was done in her life. And because she sewed, revival swept through her city. We're still talking about it today! Because Tabitha sewed.

As you take a look at your life, your job, your family, yourself, you may be tempted to despair. Your capacity may not be equal to your destiny or your opportunity. But what do you have? What skills, virtues, and resources do you have that God might use? Do not underestimate what God can do with the little that you have. God can use it to transform not just your own life, but that of your family, your church, and even your country.

Jacob was a sneak and a liar. His family was a mess. But God was going to use him to restore all of that. You might be in the middle of a mess too. But ignoring it will do you no good. You must face up to the truth so that you can set about doing what must be done. Failing to take prophetic stock of what's right in front of you could lead to terrible error. You'll never get across that sea if you can't determine your position.

The good news is, God's Holy Spirit is ready to help you. He can show you what needs work, and what is just not working. And then He can take that staff in your hand and do miracles with it. Take stock of your life, look around with both eyes open, and be honest with yourself. This is a hard step, but don't worry – it's only the first step!

STUDY QUESTIONS

1.) Have you ever felt the pressure of potential? How did you handle it? Do you wish you had handled it differently?

2.) Is it strange to think of Jacob's family as so dysfunctional? Are any of these personalities or conflicts familiar to you?

3.) Are you more like Esau, the wild child, or Jacob the sneaky rule-follower? How would you describe your personality? What are your strengths and weaknesses?

4.) Why is God so focused on truth? How have you justified lies or half-truths? What might it feel like to live a totally honest life?

5.) How do you relate to the woman at the well? Have you ever had someone speak hard truth to you? How do most people react when God sends a prophet to confront them?

6.) Do you agree that ignoring uncomfortable truths is a bad idea? Why does it often take a major crash for us to admit our shortcomings?

Struggle & Surrender

7.) What situations are you in that are concealing trouble? Think of your relationships, your workplace, your church, your community, your nation. What hard truths do you need to admit?

8.) Have you ever felt like Simon Peter, when your self-perception was painfully corrected? How did you respond in that moment? How did you benefit from it?

9.) Do you feel like your life is too small to make a difference? Are you encouraged by the story of Tabitha? Daydream a little about how God might be able to use your life.

10.) After reading this chapter, what changes do you think God might want to make through the reading of this book? Make that issue a point of prayer as you continue reading.

3

THE BREAKING POINT

JACOB'S DECEPTION

(Genesis 27:1-41)

DEFINING MOMENTS

Can you think of any defining moments from your life? These are moments that mark a change; after this, life will never be the same. If you had to tell your life's story quickly, these are the moments that you couldn't skip. They might be loud and exciting, or they could be quiet and internal. Our lives are divided into seasons, and these moments are the pivot points between them. Change may not come right away, but after you've had a defining moment, change is coming, no doubt about it.

Look at the history of America for example. The arrival of the first ships at Jamestown or Plymouth was a point of no return. The American Revolution was another such point, composed of smaller points: the Boston Tea Party, the signing of the Declaration of

Independence, Washington's victory at Yorktown. We might add the ratification of the Constitution, the Civil War, World War II, MLK's March on Washington, and so on.

I myself can point to a few defining moments in my own life. My family's move to Virginia when I was a baby. My call to pastoral ministry. Meeting my wife, Catlyn. The decision to plant the church in Alabama. All of these moments were disruptive and even destructive: whatever "normal" had been, it would be no longer.

We have accepted that God has a plan for us, and we have acknowledged the reality of where we are right now. The journey from here to there will not be an easy one, but we must make a beginning. There must be a defining moment that pushes you outward, away from the way things are into the way things ought to be.

Most of the time, these moments are not pleasant or fun. They are like the bombing of Pearl Harbor or the fall of Rome. You may be reading this book because of such a moment. Something has rocked your world: the death of a loved one, a divorce, getting fired from your job, being caught in a lie. Jacob's defining moment was one he would regret for the rest of his life.

But God allows and even initiates defining moments in order to prod us out of our comfort zone. When we understand what these moments are, and what their function could be, we can embrace the sudden chaos and make a change. You're already in the storm, why not take the wheel and steer this ship to safety? Or better yet – let Jesus take the wheel?

And there's one more thing to know: You can have a defining moment any time you like. You need not (and should not) wait for the economy or your girlfriend to shove you out into the action. Don't wait for the car to break down, take it in for some preventative maintenance. It may be too late for that, but the time to make a change is when you recognize the need for one.

If your heart is stirring after taking honest stock of your life, then it's go-time. That stirring comes from the Holy Spirit. He's trying to lead you out into the wilderness. Let this be your defining moment

NORMAL BREAKS NORMAL

We've already seen the "normal" life of Jacob and his family, and it's not great. Mom and dad each have their favorite kid, and their former romance has cooled. Big Red (Esau) is a hellraiser and a troublemaker, while precious Jacob is domesticated, manipulative and sneaky. These kinds of situations can last for a long time, but they only ever end in a crash. We look back at the financial situation prior to 2008 and wonder not why things went bust, but why it took so long.

Genesis 27 moves the story forward to, "When Isaac was old and his eyes were dim so that he could not see". He called Esau to him and said, "Behold, I am old; I do not know the day of my death." Isaac would have been between 100 and 130 years old here. That's old, but he would live to be 180, so this was not yet his time to go. Perhaps he was terribly sick and worried, or maybe Isaac was just a hypochondriac. Whatever the case, he sent Esau to hunt so that he could eat one last meal, "That my soul may bless you before I die." Esau went.

But "Rebekah was listening" without Jacob's knowledge. And not only did she eavesdrop, she failed to confront her husband on his deception. Remember, God had promised them that Esau would serve Jacob, and Jacob had purchased Esau's birthright. Isaac was trying to favor his oldest son without anyone else knowing about it. And Esau was taking this chance to recover the birthright that he had so foolishly (but legally) given up. You'd think Rebekah would storm in and have it out. But instead, she waited for Esau to leave, and filled Jacob in on the situation.

And this woman coached her son in the art of manipulation and trickery. Jacob would have a hard time later with women pushing him around, and it's easy to see where it began.

> "Go to the flock," she said, "and bring me two good young goats, so that I may prepare from them delicious food for your father, such as he loves. And you shall bring it to your father to eat, so that he may bless you before he dies." (Genesis 27:9-10)

Jacob pointed out the obvious problem, that he looked nothing like Esau. Even his blind father would be able to recognize his smooth skin and clean scent. Well, Rebekah had that covered too:

> "Rebekah took the best garments of Esau her older son, which were with her in the house, and put them on Jacob her younger son. And the skins of the young goats she put on his hands and on the smooth part of his neck" (Genesis 27:15-16).

They are going to take advantage of an old, sick, blind man in order to secure an inheritance.

You probably know the story. Jacob went in to see his father, and Isaac was immediately suspicious. He wondered how Esau could have gotten back so quickly, and insisted that Jacob draw near.

> "So Jacob went near to Isaac his father, who felt him and said, 'The voice is Jacob's voice, but the hands are the hands of Esau.'" (Genesis 27:22)

How hairy was this guy if his dad couldn't tell the difference between him and goat fur?

But Isaac asked him one more time, "Are you really my son Esau?" and Jacob lied, "I am" (Genesis 27:24). So Isaac ate the food and pronounced the patriarchal blessing upon him. This was no mere hopeful wish, this was an official and spiritual passing-on of the inheritance of the firstborn, as well as the Promise that God had made to Abraham. This would have been as legally binding as a contract is today. Jacob had gotten what he wanted, so he left his father's side.

Of course, when Esau returned, the whole thing came out. Isaac "trembled very violently" and Esau "cried out with an exceedingly great and bitter cry" (Genesis 27:33-34). But Isaac could only provide a lesser blessing for his oldest son. Esau flew into a rage:

> "Is he not rightly named Jacob? For he has cheated me these two times. He took away my birthright, and behold, now he has taken away my blessing." (Genesis 27:36)

Remember, "Jacob" means "Heel-Catcher", referring to treachery and lies. Esau fumed that Jacob was living up to his name and reputation. Indeed, they all were. And Esau swore to his brother that the moment their father died, he would kill him and take the blessing anyway (Genesis 27:41).

These problems had been festering for a long time. Esau was a hothead. Isaac was a glutton. Rebekah was a shrew. Jacob was a master manipulator. They competed and they schemed, and now it had gone too far. Matters were far worse for Jacob now, and there was no going back. One way or another, he had reached a defining moment in his life.

CONFLICT, CRISIS AND CONSCIENCE

When I was a Freshman at Liberty University, I bounced around between two different majors: Electrical Engineering and Computer Science. I was not especially passionate about either one. But I figured if I was going to work a miserable job the rest of my life, I might as well make money. That second semester was awful. My grades were fine, and the work was interesting enough, but I wanted to quit. Problem was, nothing else on the list of possible majors excited me either. I simply could not get over the fact that nothing on that list would have any value after I died. Morbid thoughts for a college student. "Vanity of vanities!" I cried, "All is vanity!" (Ecclesiastes 1:2)

One day, I couldn't take it another minute, so I cut Calculus and went to the park. I could take you to the very parking space where I was sitting, up by the tennis courts. As I sat in the car, I prayed, asking God for direction in my life. And I remember reading Matthew 9:37-38, where Jesus said,

"The harvest is plentiful, but the laborers are few; therefore pray earnestly to the Lord of the harvest to send out laborers into his harvest."

I read that and then prayed out loud, "Lord, I don't want to pray for laborers, I want to *be* a laborer!"

I stopped cold. That had come out of my mouth! I had never considered pastoral ministry, but there it was, spilling out of my heart. God had finally allowed me to recognize the call on my life. I spent the rest of the day walking the trails, soaking in this new realization. When I had driven into that parking lot, I had no idea that it would become the scene of my defining moment.

God has a life planned for us, and the life we are living right now does not measure up to it. So in big and small ways, the Holy Spirit will bring us to moments of truth, when we must set out on the journey of transformation. The moment that broke Jacob's family was not an isolated incident, but the culmination of years of deception and favoritism. The moment that led me to the pastorate was the culmination of a period of frustration and aimlessness. When "normal" builds up, it bursts, and that disruption can lead to positive change.

There are three ways that a breaking point can come into your life. The first is through internal pressure. That's the story of Jacob. No great calamity struck his family, it was his own deceit that caused the problem. When bad habits cause disastrous consequences, or when a toxic relationship blows up, you have reached a breaking point. Your life is thrown into upheaval. This is like ancient warfare, when sappers would dig under the wall and undermine the enemy's foundations. The fall seems to happen all at once, but it has been a long time in the making.

The second way is through external catastrophe. If the first way is a negative experience, this one is neutral. That doesn't make it enjoyable, it just means you might not be to blame. War, famine, death, natural disaster – all these things are external catastrophes that break "normal". When Hurricane Katrina struck New Orleans, a lot of people, through no fault of their own, reached a defining moment and were forced to embark on a journey of growth. External catastrophes often serve to reveal pre-existing spiritual problems and thereby trigger an internal breaking point as well.

The third way is the best way. You can reach a defining moment through spiritual courage. When nothing has broken or crashed, but you know that something is not right, and you decide to step out and grow, you have reached a defining moment. The benefit here is that you are not under the pressure of a crisis, and you can move forward thoughtfully.

God is a good Father and a wise Teacher. He sees us and knows what He needs us to be to fulfill His plan. For that reason, He will try to lead you to a defining moment. It starts with gentle nudges in the spirit: a sermon at church or a thought that seems to come out of nowhere. He'll put you in situations where your misaligned thoughts and attitudes are likely to flare up. And God is even gracious enough to send crises into our lives to get our attention.

Every crisis, every conflict, every moment of conscience can become a turning point in your life. Put another way: every one of these things is already a turning point. The only question is which way you are going to turn.

BATTLING INERTIA

Nobody likes being disrupted. We are creatures of habit, and subject to the law of inertia. An object at rest will stay at rest, and so will a person living their version of "normal". Even if "normal" is horrible, we like it because it is familiar. It is known territory, and we are more afraid of what might be out there than the mess we have learned to manage. Many victims of physical abuse will stay for a lifetime because the only thing more frightening than their attacker is the world outside their home. For this reason, we resist our defining moments. We postpone growth for rain, snow or sunshine. But if we are being honest, we know that this is foolish.

Here's an extreme example, but it's a perfect illustration of our human reluctance to get going. The children of Israel cried out to God for rescue from their slavery in Egypt (Exodus 2:23). God sent Moses to come and speak to Pharaoh. The people were enthusiastic at first (Exodus 4:31), but when their workload was increased, they cursed Moses (Exodus 5:21). Then when they were out of Egypt by the sea, they panicked as they saw Pharaoh's chariots approaching (Exodus 14:11-12). They wanted freedom, but they lacked the courage to step away from the slavery they had always known. And had God not supported Moses, they would have chosen to go back and submit to their taskmasters. We face the same temptation.

But you know things cannot stay the same. Your financial irresponsibility is unsustainable. Your lack of communication with your husband cannot continue. Your bitterness towards your mother is going to manifest someday. Your secret sins will wreck your testimony. In the World War II series, *Band of Brothers*, the naïve Lieutenant Dyke panics as he leads his men in an assault. He freezes and hides behind a haystack as the bullets whiz by. "Go forward!" shouts Major Winters. "We cannot stay here!" beg his men, "We have to keep moving!" Forward is the only way to go, even if it scares you to death.

Maybe you've had your defining moment, or you're in the middle of it now, and that's why you're reading this. Perhaps there has been a blowup like Jacob's. Your marriage that seemed so stable is on the verge of dissolution because of your spending habits. Or maybe you always knuckle under to your boss, and now other relationships are at risk because of your cowardice.

Perhaps it's an external catastrophe. You've been laid off, a child has died, you've received a cancer diagnosis, the country has gone to war. You are being forced to change, even though you'd rather not.

Then again, perhaps you have chosen to take a step of spiritual courage. You know that your big mouth is going to get you into trouble someday, so you have determined to do something about it. You're going to put down that bottle before you lose your family. Or maybe you've committed to finding a new job and relaunching your career. Any of these can be defining moments.

Of course, you could choose to reject your turning point. The army of Israel marched out to face Goliath every day for forty days only to turn tail and run when they got a fresh look at his face (1 Samuel 17:20-24). Are you intimidated by the prospect of change and growth? There is nothing wrong with fear, but you mustn't let it master you. Yes, it's intimidating to face down your boss, but can you really go back to your desk and start falsifying financial reports? You might not know how to spend your time apart from pornography, but are you going to jeopardize your marriage for something so childish?

Not only that, but there is really no way to go back after you've come to a defining moment. Once you lie to steal your brother's blessing, you cannot un-lie and un-steal. This is especially true of major crises. When the nation is invaded, or the economy collapses, wishing and hoping that such things had not happened will do you little good. The same is true of self-realization. Now that you know that your quiet demeanor is a cloak for arrogance, can you ignore that truth about yourself? And good luck trying to take a friendship back to where it used to be, after a knock-down drag-out fight.

If you decide to reject the defining moment and return to Egypt, so to speak, you will lose what little good you already had. The Jews hated Rome and wanted them gone, so the Lord sent Jesus as their Messiah. But they could not let go of their traditions or their position. "We have no king but Caesar," they told Pontius Pilate (John 19:15). Once they had met Jesus, there was no going back, except as subjects of the hated emperor. You can't ignore it when the moment comes, not without losing something.

Or you could have a defining moment right now. You need not wait until Esau threatens to kill you, or a tornado blows through your backyard. You can choose to break "normal" right now. That is, by far, the best way to do it. And if you're already in the maelstrom of decision, you might as well leverage that chaos to make some positive spiritual changes.

FACING THE MUSIC

The Bible usually introduces its heroes at their pivot point. There are a few exceptions, but the story often begins at the moment that will launch them forward into their calling

Sometimes the moment comes crashing through the door as an external crisis. Daniel and his companions are examples of this. They were living in Jerusalem during the siege and were taken hostage back to Babylon. The king intended to train up the Hebrew nobility in the ways of Babylon to consolidate power and ensure Jewish loyalty. He gave them the best of everything, even letting them eat from his own table, which included partaking of unclean foods. Daniel had done nothing wrong, but the moment had come to make a decision, ready or not. "Daniel resolved that he would not defile himself," the Bible tells us (Daniel 1:8). He determined in that moment that he would obey the Lord and let the crisis shape him into a man of strength and faith, even if it cost him his life.

Joseph was in a similar position. Interpretations differ over Joseph's character as a young man. I'm inclined to think that he was a spoiled kid who drove his half-brothers crazy with his attitude. Either way, he was thrown into a pit and sold by his own family into slavery. From the moment he arrives in Egypt, we only see Joseph as a wise, righteous man. Whether he needed to learn some humility along the way, or whether he had already learned it, Joseph allowed God to leverage the crisis in his life to make him a better man.

How about Saul of Tarsus? His defining moment was very dramatic. He had been a zealous persecutor of the Church, giving approval to the death of Stephen, the first martyr (Acts 7:58). On the road to Damascus, where he had been given authority to arrest more Christians, God shone a blinding light upon him and knocked him to the ground. With a loud voice, He called, "Saul, Saul, why are you persecuting me?" (Acts 9:4). For three days he was blind, in fasting and prayer. Everything Saul had believed about Jesus was wrong. He submitted to God and became Paul the apostle.

Now, you might think that if God knocked you off of your horse and shone a bright light in your face, you'd be willing to change too. But you underestimate the stubbornness of people. Every day, men and women reject the call of God to leave behind the old "normal" and move forward.

Consider Ahab. Ahab was the most wicked king the northern kingdom of Israel ever had (1 Kings 16:33). He married the Sidonian princess, Jezebel, who established the worship of Baal and killed the Lord's prophets. Ahab's most famous failure was when he had Naboth the Jezreelite killed in a mock trial so that he could have his vineyard (1 Kings 21:16). Elijah the prophet appeared to him and prophesied that both he and his queen would die, and their blood be lapped up by the dogs (1 Kings 21:23-24).

> "And when Ahab heard these words, he tore his clothes and put sackcloth on his flesh and lay in sackcloth and went about dejectedly." (1 Kings 21:27)

Ahab's repentance was so moving that God promised to delay the judgment upon his house until after his death (1 Kings 21:29). This could have been a wonderful tale of restoration, but it is not.

69

In the very next chapter, we see Ahab celebrating with Jehoshaphat the king of Judah, likely to seal their marriage alliance between Jehoshaphat's son and his daughter Athaliah. Ahab has the idea to go to war together, but the righteous Jehoshaphat wants to inquire of the Lord first. Ahab brings in four hundred prophets who predict that they will rout the Syrians at Ramoth-gilead in spectacular fashion. But Jehoshaphat knows something is suspicious about these so-called men of God.

Ahab reveals that he has another prophet in prison, Micaiah, imprisoned for prophesying bad news against him (1 Kings 22:8). Ahab has learned nothing from his big moment. He is still manipulating religion to suit his own ends. Micaiah announced the fulfillment of Elijah's prophecy, and Ahab died in the battle at Ramoth-gilead. The dogs lapped up the blood from his chariot (1 Kings 22:38). By failing to take advantage of his defining moment, Ahab was unable to escape the doom that God had warned him about. Miss the moment, and you end up worse off than before.

As always, Jesus is our greatest example. He had come from Heaven to die on the cross. But when the moment came, He was scared to death.

> "Father," He prayed, "if it be possible, let this cup pass from me; nevertheless, not as I will, but as you will." (Matthew 26:39)

Jesus embraced the defining moment of history, even though it would come at great personal cost and pain. Are you prepared to do the same?

THIS MOMENT CONTAINS ALL MOMENTS

C.S. Lewis wrote a fascinating book called *The Great Divorce*. In it, souls from Hell have an opportunity to visit Heaven. They are each given one final chance to embrace the Gospel. It's a remarkable story that illustrates the kinds of petty things that keep people from repentance. In one story, a man with a lizard on his shoulder, representing his lust, faces down an angel who tells him that in order to enter the Kingdom, he must allow that lizard to be killed. The man panics as the creature whispers in his ear, and says he will come back and do it another day. "There is no other day," says the angel, "All days are present now. This moment contains all moments."

I love that line. "This moment contains all moments." God loves to bring us to life's hinges. For Jacob, it was the discovery of his deception by Esau and his father. There was no going back. In a sense, every moment of his life was contained in that moment when his tricks were discovered.

You've had moments like that. But perhaps you have allowed them to pass you by. You ducked your head and waited out the storm. Now matters are worse, and you haven't changed a bit. If that's true, then you have left yourself wide open to another blowup, because nothing has changed in the most important area – yourself.

If you're in the middle of a catastrophe like a job loss or a natural disaster, let it drive you towards the Lord. He wants to use this moment to shape you into someone who can handle such crises better. If your situation is more like Jacob's, and the mess is one that you have made yourself, then you really need to take stock and make this moment count. As Winston Churchill said, "Never let a good crisis go to waste." In the clamor of uncertainty, we are more teachable, and so God allows these times to come.

But there is nothing stopping you from making this day, this hour, this minute, one of the pivot points of your life. The Holy Spirit is constantly drawing us to embark on the journey of sanctification. You don't need to be at a special church meeting, or coming out of a major sickness, or worrying about your rebellious kids to meet God and make a change. You know what's not right in your life, so will you choose to do something about it?

"Normal" is no good, because 'normal" does not live up to the glory God has prepared for you. Whether it has already blown up, or whether you need to blow it up,

> "Today, if you hear his voice, do not harden your hearts."
> (Hebrews 3:7-8)

STUDY QUESTIONS

1.) What have been the defining moments in your life? Were these positive or negative experiences?

2.) What do you think about the idea that you could have a defining moment any time you like? Is this better or worse than waiting for one to happen to you?

3.) Are you surprised by the state of Isaac and Rebekah's marriage? What do you think their relationship was like after this?

4.) Can you see how the crisis in Jacob's family was inevitable by the way everyone was acting? What might have been done to prevent such a situation?

5.) Defining moments come through: internal pressure, external catastrophe, or spiritual courage. Can you think of examples in life, the Bible or pop culture that illustrate each of these?

6.) Have you ever gone through a terrible situation only to be grateful for it later? What does that say about the wisdom of God?

7.) Have you ever refused to learn your lesson in a crisis? What could you have done differently?

8.) Have you ever used spirituality to conceal you lack of a heart change after a crisis? Why is this a bad idea?

9.) Consider the example from *The Great Divorce* – "This moment contains all moments". Does it intimidate you to change your life, even for the better?

10.) Are you ready to have a defining moment? Are you already in the middle of one? Determine in your heart that you will emerge from this realization a new man or woman, by the grace of God.

4

INTO THE WILDERNESS

THE FLIGHT OF JACOB

(Genesis 27:42-28:9)

A VOICE CRYING OUT

Let's imagine you are living in Judea around 30 A.D. You have gone to the Jordan River to draw water, or swim, or wash your clothes. When out of the desert comes a man with wild, mangy hair. He goes to the water and begins to shout:

"Repent, for the kingdom of heaven is at hand!" (Matthew 3:2)

He calls out the sins of the nation with incisive courage. As you look on, a man comes forward, asking what he must do. The wild man takes the individual, and after a short conference, dunks him under the water. John the Baptist has begun his ministry.

Born into a priestly family, John was raised a Nazirite, which means he never cut his hair, he never tasted wine or grapes, and he abstained from everyday forms of uncleanness. At some point, John grew impatient with the corruption of the nation, especially the priesthood, and he went to the desert.

> "Now John was clothed with camel's hair and wore a leather belt around his waist and ate locusts and wild honey." (Mark 1:6)

There he learned the voice of the Lord, and the Holy Spirit, who was in him from birth, gave him his mission. This man, the last of the Old Covenant prophets, was the fulfillment of Isaiah 40:3,

> "A voice cries, 'In the wilderness prepare the way of the Lord; make straight in the desert a highway for our God.'"

John the Baptist was a man of the wilderness. It was his home, his natural habitat. And for that reason, his life is instructive for us. The Holy Spirit of God identifies our shortcomings and immaturities and brings us to a turning point. But where do we go after that moment of truth? To the wilderness. God calls each of His children there, because that is where He may be found.

The wilderness is a place of deprivation and hardship. There are no modern amenities or kind faces. If I can use a *Star Wars* example, the wilderness is like the cave Luke Skywalker explored during his training on Dagobah. "What's in there?" he asked. Yoda replied, "Only what you take with you." The wilderness is a place of unfiltered reality, where there is nowhere to hide from God or from yourself. It's a hard place, but it's where you need to be.

John called his countrymen to leave behind their sinful lives, and step up into their God-given destiny as His chosen people. He baptized them and sent them back to make things right. His voice cries out still. If you are fed up with your own corruption, or the sins of your nation, or the malaise over your church, it is time to enter the wilderness. You might come out looking a little strange, like John did. You might attract some angry attention; John surely did. And you might even suffer for it, as did John. But it's a journey that must be taken if you desire to realize the purpose of God for your life.

INTO THE UNKNOWN

Our story continues,

"The words of Esau her older son were told to Rebekah. So she sent and called Jacob her younger son and said to him...Arise, flee to Laban my brother in Haran and stay with him for a while, until your brother's fury turns away." (Genesis 27:42-44)

You have to wonder what Rebekah's plan had been once Esau and Isaac discovered her deception. Perhaps she thought Esau would meekly accept the new turn of events. But Esau's hotblooded nature was roused and aimed at his brother, and Rebekah was worried. Remember, Isaac would live for a long time to come, but no one at this point knew that. So Rebekah determined to send Jacob away, out of Esau's murderous reach.

Haran was Rebekah's hometown. It had been Abraham's last stop before his final journey to the Promised Land, and many of their clan still lived there. Abraham had sent his servant to Haran to find a wife for Isaac rather than wed him to one of the idolatrous Canaanites. That was where we first met Rebekah, where she watered the camels of the servant in answer to his prayer. It was also where we first met Laban, her crafty brother. And that is where Jacob is being sent to join his family.

Rebekah complained of Esau's Hittite wives and convinced Isaac to send Jacob away to find a bride (Genesis 27:46). Once again, the son of Promise comes across as the pawn of his wife, apparently unconcerned by the coming conflict between his twin boys. But Isaac acceded to the plan and blessed Jacob once again.

"Thus Isaac sent Jacob away. And he went to Paddan-aram, to Laban." (Genesis 28:5)

The family is disintegrating. Esau had been foolish with his birthright, but was too proud to accept his loss, turning his violent aggression on his twin. Isaac had been deaf to the Word of the Lord concerning his sons and had provoked them by his lack of leadership. Rebekah had schemed to get her favorite son the pride of place, and had now lost them both. She would never see Jacob again. And Jacob, who had let himself be pushed into lying and cheating, was forced to flee from his own home into the wilderness.

It was a long journey to Haran, and it seems Jacob went alone. Away from his mother and father. Away from his twin brother. Away from the Promised Land. Away from the bountiful life he had enjoyed as the son of a wealthy sheikh. Into the unknown. Remember, Jacob was a quiet, domestic type. He enjoyed tents, the indoors. Esau was the hunter, the woodsman. But now Jacob was forced away from everything comfortable to make a long journey. Doubtless he was full of shame at his own sin, full of fear of the retribution of his brother, and full of anger at himself for letting things go so far. That journey was Jacob's entrée into the literal and spiritual wilderness.

There's another tacked-on anecdote before the narrative moves on. It says,

> "When Esau saw that the Canaanite women did not please Isaac his father, Esau went to Ishmael and took as his wife, besides the wives he had, Mahalath, the daughter of Ishmael, Abraham's son, the sister of Nebaioth." (Genesis 28:8-9)

Esau cuts a pathetic figure in these verses. He went and acquired a wife from the line of Abraham – his parents' excuse for sending Jacob away – so that he might earn their love. It's enough to break your heart. This family was competitive and selfish, and these grown men were taking drastic steps to please their parents. Esau was a carnal man, but we can certainly sympathize with his sorrows.

Truly, the whole family was in the wilderness now. "Normal" was broken, and everything was in a state of upheaval. Things were going to change; there was no turning back. Jacob was leaving behind a terrible mess. But it is only the beginning of his story. God would use that wilderness to shape Jacob into a man who could return and bring order and righteousness to that disaster.

GOD'S TRAINING GROUND

The wilderness is one of the most powerful and common symbols in the Bible. It is the space outside the city walls, the vast stretches of desert that separated the settlements in the Ancient Near East. For that reason, it became a symbol of the unknown, the unfamiliar. It is the domain of wild beasts, scorpions and carrion birds, therefore also a symbol of danger and death. And it is a place of solitude and silence, away from the corruption of the cities. It is a picture of primitive aloneness, the ideal place to hear the voice of God.

This idea is not unique to the world of the Bible. Many cultures have symbolic meaning attached to the wilderness: the desert, the forest, the swamp, the cave, or the sea. Native American tribes would send their young men into the forest alone for initiation into adulthood. Arabian cultures have a fear and respect for the open desert as a place full of danger and mystery.

Even in pop culture do we see such wilderness imagery. Bilbo Baggins is at home in the Shire, a cultivated, gardenlike country, but is forced out into a world full of forests and mountains. When Simba flees from his uncle Scar, he goes out into the desert and nearly perishes on the journey. Stephen Sondheim's musical, *Into the Woods*, uses the forest as a metaphor for change and wishes. The wilderness is a near-universal human image, which is why the Bible uses it.

Very often in Scripture, the heroes of the faith spent time in the wilderness. This is not just poetry. God would quite literally take His champions out from among other men, away from the trouble He was calling them to fix, and take them to the desert. When Jesus Himself was baptized, signaling the beginning of His ministry, "The Spirit immediately drove him out into the wilderness" (Mark 1:12). These journeys are times of change and preparation.

Of course, when we think of the wilderness, our thoughts immediately rush to the children of Israel, who wandered in the wilderness for forty years under Moses. Have you ever wondered why God led them there first, instead of directly to the Promised Land?

Well, at the end of those forty years, just before they crossed the Jordan, Moses told them why:

> "You shall remember the whole way that the Lord your God has led you these forty years in the wilderness, that he might humble you, testing you to know what was in your heart, whether you would keep his commandments or not. And he humbled you and let you hunger and fed you with manna, which you did not know, nor did your fathers know, that he might make you know that man does not live by bread alone, but man lives by every word that comes from the mouth of the Lord. Your clothing did not wear out on you and your foot did not swell these forty years. Know then in your heart that, as a man disciplines his son, the Lord your God disciplines you. So you shall keep the commandments of the Lord your God by walking in his ways and by fearing him. For the Lord your God is bringing you into a good land, a land of brooks of water, of fountains and springs, flowing out in the valleys and hills." (Deuteronomy 8:2-7)

Moses calls them to remember those long decades in the wilderness as motivation for keeping God's commandments in the Promised Land. And he gives the reason why God put them through that ordeal. First, he says it was to humble them. Second, it was to test them. And in verse 5, he summarizes the whole process as the discipline of the Lord, such as a father brings upon his son. Don't just think of discipline in terms of punishment, but like a drill sergeant making soldiers out of raw recruits.

That is the purpose of the wilderness. God uses the wilderness as His training ground. First, He humbles us. Consider the image. When you are deprived of something like water or food or human company, you very quickly realize who you are. Today we like to talk about getting "hangry" when dinner is delayed. Imagine being without food in the forest, or on the frozen tundra. You would soon lose any refinement you might have in society. Soldiers serving under George Washington ate their own leather shoes during the harsh winter in Valley Forge. The first thing God does in the wilderness is He breaks you down. He strings us out until we have lost all pretense and sophistication. Jesus fasted in the wilderness for forty days before the temptation came (Matthew 4:2).

And that's the next thing we see: God tests us in the wilderness. Once He has brought us to the end of ourselves, He allows us to be tested to see if we are going to keep His commandments. The children of Israel were without bread and water at times. God was testing them to see if they would trust His promises and keep His commandments or not. They very frequently failed these tests and were forced to go back for remedial training. Navy SEALs go through a long, rigorous training program. They are expected to perform at a high level under lack of sleep, sore muscles, difficult conditions, and sadistic instructors. This is to see if they will be able to do the real job under such pressures. God does the same for us. Like the widow at Zarephath, He waits until there is only one portion of oil left before He asks us to give Him some (1 Kings 17). Jesus was hungry when Satan tempted Him to turn the loaves into bread. He passed the test by quoting from Deuteronomy 8, the passage we just read (Matthew 4:2-4).

That is the discipline of the Lord, as symbolized by the wilderness. It is His school of hard knocks, where He makes men out of the boys who come to Him. And it need not be a literal wilderness (although there is value there). Any time your world collapses, you are in the wilderness. When your relationships crumble, you are in the wilderness. In times of war, or famine, or economic depression, we are in the wilderness. During those seasons we are made into the people God can use. But you can also enter the wilderness voluntarily and be prepared ahead of time for those darker seasons.

Is this pleasant? No. But all of it is to prepare us for the Promised Land, the destiny that God has promised us. There are lessons that we will need when the time comes, and we learn them in the wilderness.

THE VALUE OF VOLUNTARY DISCOMFORT

One of my heroes of Church history is Anthony of Alexandria, also known as St. Anthony or Anthony the Great. He was born a wealthy man, but sold all that he had to go and live in the desert. He was not the first monk, but he was the catalyst of the movement. He ate next to nothing, he lived alone, and he would spend long vigils in prayer without sleep. His goal was to achieve total mastery over the flesh and total submission to the Spirit. And the place he found to do that was the wilderness.

Now, as a good Protestant, I tend to be skeptical of anything monastic. The word "legalism" leaps to my lips pretty quickly. But keep in mind that Anthony did not force his decision on anyone else, and certainly did not see it as necessary for salvation. In fact, he said he chose such a lifestyle because of his own sinful frailty. God would use him to strengthen the Church during times of great persecution. Because of his reputation, Roman officials were too afraid to arrest him when he returned to Alexandria. And he was the teacher of Athanasius, who would go on to rescue the Church from the Arian heresy and secure the acceptance of the Trinity.

Did Anthony do some weird things? In his later years he took to wearing a hair shirt when he grew too comfortable in the desert, so yeah. But his prayers were powerful and efficacious. He was illiterate but memorized enormous swathes of Scripture. And despite his solitary intentions, he was a mentor to countless Christians who sought him out. Anthony was a man, like John the Baptist, who knew the value of the wilderness.

As I said before, the wilderness is primarily a spiritual state, but allow me to give a brief plug for the actual wild itself. There is something to be said for getting away to nature to meet with God alone. That could be the desert, the bayou, the mountains or simply the park. I recommend turning off your phone, or leaving it behind entirely. When I lived in Virginia, there was a cabin I would visit that had no cell reception and no Wi-Fi. That was my wilderness. Yours could be the early morning hours on the beach, it doesn't matter. The point is to get to a place where it is just you and God. No distractions, no obligations.

But whether you make it to the woods or not, it is in your best interest to enter the wilderness on your own, before life forces you there. Jacob was put into the wilderness for the first time because of his deception, and it shook him up. You ought to be familiar with that territory so that when life happens, you know what to do. Those who study every day need not panic when midterms roll around, but folks like me who tend to procrastinate are left to cram the night before. There's no sense in showing up for the football game if you haven't run a few wind sprints before the big day. Preparation needs to happen beforehand, or you will get knocked down too easily.

How do we do this? Through what we call the spiritual disciplines. Remember, the purpose of the wilderness is discipline, humbling and testing. The spiritual disciplines are how we engage in that process. None of these things are new to you, and none of them are very exciting. But much like wind sprints, they are exactly what is needed to build your strength for the coming ordeal. I'll just list a few.

Most obvious is prayer. Prayer is the act of speaking to God. It can take the form of worship, confession, intercession (praying for someone else), supplication (praying for yourself), or thanksgiving. There is really no secret to prayer. It's not the act itself that is difficult, it is the focus to kneel down and do it that is so often lacking. But Paul told the Thessalonians to "Pray without ceasing" (1 Thessalonians 5:17). Through prayer we open a conversation with God that can continue through good times and bad.

The other big one is the Bible. Read your Bible! That book has changed lives, uprooted kingdoms and withstood all opposition, just think of what it might do for you (Hebrews 4:12). If every word of that Bible is true, and if it really came from God, then you ought to know what's in it. Learn how God has dealt with other men and learn how He will deal with you. Read it, memorize it, study it, and treasure it in your heart.

Fasting is often associated with the wilderness. Try abstaining from food for a time. Usually this is done sundown to sundown. Eat supper, and then skip breakfast, lunch and snacks until the next day's supper. Instead, pray and study your Bible during that time. Jesus assumed that His disciples would fast (Mark 2:20), so we ought to do it. Don't just fast from food, take a break from TV, secular music, or social media. You just might break those things' hold over you.

I could go on to talk about meditation, tithing, evangelism, service and more. None of these things are much fun, are they? But there is value in voluntary discomfort. The spiritual disciplines are there to train you. They prepare you for the times when God and His Word are the only things you have to cling to.

"Practice these things, immerse yourself in them, so that all may see your progress." (1 Timothy 4:15)

Discipline yourself during the in-between so that when the test comes, you are prepared. Even the world can see the value of taking time every day to be quiet and take a break from luxury. How much more should we, who have a spiritual mandate to do so?

You will not always have the choice to enter the wilderness. You might be there now because of something you've done, or something that was done to you. Your question now becomes: Will you allow God to humble, test and discipline you during this time? Or will you break under the strain and find yourself worse off than before? I hope you will embrace the discomfort of the wilderness. God wants to teach you something. Something you can only learn here. Something that you must know if you ever want to see His calling on your life fulfilled.

NOTABLE ALUMNI

Whether you have entered the wilderness voluntarily or not, you will find yourself in good company. All of God's greatest champions have spent time in the wilderness. There the Holy Spirit trains them for their mission, equipping them with everything they will need for the battle ahead.

Moses was sent to the wilderness involuntarily. We've already told his story, with his presumptuous swagger. When he tried to settle a dispute between two Hebrews, they rebuffed him and threw his shortcomings in his face. He was forced to flee into the Sinai desert and then to Midian. He spent forty years there as a shepherd, a job detestable to any Egyptian (Genesis 46:34). When God finally called to him from the burning bush, Moses had learned humility (Exodus 3:11).

Later on, he would be known as the meekest man on the earth (Numbers 12:3). After four decades in the wilderness, he was ready for God to use him.

Paul was a mix in terms of his willingness to enter the wilderness. On the road to Damascus, he was knocked down by a blinding light and the voice of God spoke to him (Acts 9:4). After three days of blindness, Paul became a Christian and was baptized. After that happened, he said later,

> "I went away into Arabia, and returned again to Damascus." (Galatians 1:17)

Paul spent about three years in the wilderness, communing with the Holy Spirit, and receiving the revelation of the Gospel that he would preach to the Gentiles. He would never have gone there on his own. But when he realized the truth, Paul went straight to the desert.

Elijah had two trips to the wilderness. The first time was after he announced the three-year drought to King Ahab. God then told him,

> "Depart from here and turn eastward and hide yourself by the brook Cherith, which is east of the Jordan. You shall drink from the brook, and I have commanded the ravens to feed you there." (1 Kings 17:3-4)

Elijah was alone at the brook for years; in prayer, in study of the Law, and observing daily miracles. Then after his great victory, when he called down fire from Heaven, Queen Jezebel announced her intention to kill him. Out of fear, Elijah fled back to the wilderness, where God would strengthen him again to continue the mission (1

Kings 19). First he learned miraculous faith, and then he learned courage. Elijah would not have been the prophet we know were it not for the wilderness. At the end, it would be in the wilderness across the Jordan that he would ascend to Heaven in a chariot of fire (2 Kings 2).

But if there is an Old Testament champion of the wilderness, that honor must go to David. Like John the Baptist, the wilderness was David's natural habitat. He began life tending his father's sheep in the pasture. It was there that he penned those beautiful psalms, as he learned contentment in the Lord alone. There he learned to fight lions and bears, preparation for the giant Goliath. When Saul sought his death, he fled to the wilderness with his mighty men, where they eluded capture and fought countless battles. So much of David's poetry is replete with wilderness imagery:

> "O God, you are my God; earnestly I seek you; my soul thirst for you; my flesh faints for you, as in a dry and weary land where there is no water." (Psalm 63:1)

It was in the wilderness that the man after God's own heart learned to trust the Lord for every victory.

And if David, the champion of the wilderness, was a man after God's own heart (1 Samuel 13:14); if John the Baptist, the desert-dweller, was the greatest man who ever lived (Matthew 11:11); and if Jesus Christ would often "withdraw to desolate places and pray" (Luke 5:16) – then we ought to imitate their example.

PREPARE THE WAY OF THE LORD

Jacob had let the mess in his family simmer for so long, it finally boiled over. His character as the Heel-Catcher built to a breaking point, and he had no choice but to flee into the wilderness. If left unattended, character flaws and little lies will erode the foundation of your life. This can only lead to a collapse. When that happens, you are in the wilderness; a desolate, lonely place. It's dangerous and uncivilized and uncomfortable. You will be humbled, and you will be tested. But if you allow God to do his work there, you will be disciplined into the kind of person that can go back to fix the damage that has been done.

God has something to teach you in the wilderness. So let the desert do its work. When things break, we see flashes of who we really are. Sometimes that realization scares us to death. But don't shy away from it. God is teaching you that you cannot do this by yourself. He wants to bring you to a place of total honesty. Much like going without water under the hot sun, the results might not be pretty. People turn nasty when the chips are down. But God is a good Father and a good Coach. He will only break you down so that He can build you back up again.

You can choose to enter the wilderness and be trained by the Holy Spirit right now. God would prefer it that way. Like John the Baptist or Jesus, it is in those times of isolation and deprivation that you learn the most. By deliberately discomfiting yourself, you will rid yourself of the need for stability and luxury. And the next time things fall apart, you will have already been to the wilderness, and you will be ready for what you find there.

There is a voice crying out in the wilderness. God is calling to you. He has a destiny for you to fulfill, a Promised Land to give you. But if you hesitate at the edge of the dark forest, you will never become all that He has made you to be. It is for that reason that God will allow disasters to drive us into the wilderness. Because it is only there that we can receive the training we need. So don't resist it. Embrace it. Choose it – today, tomorrow and every day.

STUDY QUESTIONS

1.) How would you have reacted to John the Baptist? Why did Jesus call him the greatest man who ever lived (Matthew 11:11)?

2.) Why would God send so many to the wilderness? What is it about the desert or the forest or the mountains that can shape a man of God?

3.) Do you think Jacob going away was the best decision? How might things have gone differently if he stayed? What could he have done to repair the breach?

4.) What are some prominent Bible stories that involve the wilderness? How about literature, film, or pop culture? Why is this such a powerful image for people across time?

5.) Can you think of a time when you were "in the wilderness"? How were you humbled? How were you tested? Are you glad for the experience?

6.) What did the desert monks get right? What did they get wrong? Why do you think the wilderness held such an attraction for them?

7.) Do you feel more spiritual in the great outdoors? Why is it easier to pray or read your Bible or talk about spiritual things when you are away from civilization?

8.) Which of the spiritual disciplines do you do well? Which ones could use some improvement?

9.) What can we learn from the fact that God took Elijah back into the wilderness when he was at his lowest point?

10.) Are you in the wilderness now because of your circumstances? Do you need to enter the wilderness voluntarily to correct your circumstances?

5

IF GOD MAY BE KNOWN

JACOB'S DREAM AT BETHEL

(Genesis 28:10-22)

NOTHING ELSE MATTERS

As our culture has become secularized, there has been a rise in speculative fiction. The "literature" of our day is cold and hopeless and really not much fun to read. But on the other side of the bookstore you have things like *Harry Potter*, *The Lord of the Rings*, and *Dune*. Expand that out to the screen and the list just gets longer: *Star Wars*, *Game of Thrones*, *The Avengers*. As we have convinced ourselves that the world has nothing magical or mysterious in it, we have created other worlds to scratch that supernatural itch. Now we can talk of gods and monsters and magic, but keep them at a distance. Ironically enough, it is the most scientific among us who enjoy such things the most.

The reason for this compulsion to create myths and gods is because our souls are crying out for the real thing. There is a true and living God, the world is in a vicious struggle between good and evil, and we are all a part of that great adventure. If you knew that there was more to the world than what you see, that God is real and that an epic story is being played out right in front of your eyes – how might that change your life?

I once wrote a song called "Seek It Like Silver". The title comes from Proverbs 2:4-5, which says,

> "If you seek it like silver and search for it as for hidden treasures, then you will understand the fear of the Lord and find the knowledge of God."

I wanted to compile into one song, as many Bible verses about finding God as I could. Turns out there's an awful lot of them! There's Hosea 6:3, "Let us know; let us press on to know the Lord." Or James 4:8, "Draw near to God, and he will draw near to you." Best of all is Matthew 7:7-8, when Jesus said,

> "Ask, and it will be given to you; seek, and you will find; knock, and it will be opened to you. For everyone who asks receives, and the one who seeks finds, and to the one who knocks it will be opened."

My own sentiment and conclusion is summed up in the final line of the bridge: "If God may be known, nothing else matters." As far as I am concerned, if it is possible to know God, then everything else is of such minimal importance that it does not merit comparison. If the God who created me and knows everything about me – to say nothing of

94

all the secrets of the universe – is out there looking for me, and if I can be sure to find Him if I look for Him with a sincere heart, then what am I doing sitting around here?

People climb mountains on their knees to meet God. They meditate in the snow to catch a glimpse of Him. They mutilate their bodies and take psychotropic drugs and shed innocent blood all in the pursuit of God. I get it! "If God may be known, nothing else matters." There is nothing too valuable to be lost in that pursuit.

But you can know God, and you need not take peyote in the desert to do so. God loves you like a Father, He wants you to know Him. He sent His Son to make it possible for you to have fellowship with Him. You may disbelieve, but what if it were true? Would not even the possibility of finding God be worth your entire life's devotion? It's time to stop messing around and find out. What would you think of Neo if he had taken the blue pill? Or if Bilbo had sent Gandalf away while he ate his second breakfast? God is waiting for you. He wants to show you the truth of the unseen world around you, the truth of your very own soul. Who cares if you need to get down to the Tosche Station to pick up those stupid power converters? There are bigger things at stake.

In the wilderness you will meet God. And how you respond in that moment will determine the course of your entire life.

STAIRWAY TO HEAVEN

Jacob was in the wilderness. After scheming with his mother to deceive his father and steal from his brother, he had to flee to Haran to stay with his uncle Laban. He was alone, forced to sleep out in the open in strange country. He arrived at a place called Luz, and, "taking one of the stones of the place, he put it under his head and lay down in that place to sleep" (Genesis 28:11).

Luz was seventy miles from Beersheba, so he had already covered quite a distance. But the journey to Haran was one of several hundred miles. Can you imagine the unbroken string of what-if's that filled Jacob's mind with every step? He set up camp for the night, dreading the long journey, but knowing he could never go back. He must have had a difficult time getting to sleep. But this night would change his life forever.

> "He dreamed, and behold, there was a ladder set up on the earth, and the top of it reached to heaven. And behold, the angels of God were ascending and descending on it!" (Genesis 28:12)

That word for "ladder" is *sullam*, and can refer to any structure by which a person ascends: a ladder, or a stairway, for example. In any case, Jacob had a dream of a brilliant bridge to Heaven, with angels going up and down.

And atop this stairway stood the Lord God Himself, who spoke to Jacob in the dream. "I am the Lord," He said, "the God of Abraham your father and the God of Isaac" (Genesis 28:13). He renewed the Promise that had been given to Abraham and Isaac: a Promise of land, of great descendants, and a blessing that would extend to the whole world. More than that, He promised Jacob,

> "I am with you and will keep you wherever you go, and will bring you back to this land. For I will not leave you until I have done what I have promised you." (Genesis 28:15)

No doubt these words were more precious to Jacob than lofty prophecies of a glorious future.

> "Then Jacob awoke from his sleep and said, 'Surely the Lord is in this place, and I did not know it.' And he was afraid and said, 'How awesome is this place! This is none other than the house of God, and this is the gate of heaven.'" (Genesis 28:16-17)

Jacob realized that he had, quite unintentionally, stumbled upon a spiritual hotspot. What looked to him like a barren campsite near an insignificant city, was in fact holy ground. "How awesome is this place!"

Folks at this time believed that the gods were territorial, with no power outside of their own dominion. Temples and cities were built around holy places where men believed God could be found. For example, the city of Babylon was named, "Gate of the Gods". The people there worshiped atop great structures called ziggurats, like pyramids with long stairs up the sides. It is likely with this imagery in mind that God gave Jacob the vision of a stairway to Heaven. But he was not in Babylon, or even in Beersheba, but the wilderness. What was Jacob to make of this?

By revealing the stairway to Heaven in such a desolate place, God was teaching Jacob that the whole earth is His holy place. He is perfectly capable of making Himself known anywhere. Babylon was not the "Gate of the Gods", God can open up a gate anywhere He likes! Therefore, Jacob was not alone in the wilderness. God was there. And in His mercy, God promised to be with him, to support him and sustain him, even after all he had done.

The next morning, Jacob made a monument of the stone he had slept upon, and christened that spot "Bethel", meaning "House of God". This is the name that would overtake that of Luz in later days.

> "Then Jacob made a vow, saying, 'If God will be with me and will keep me in this way that I go, and will give me bread to eat and clothing to wear, so that I come again to my father's house in peace, then the Lord shall be my God." (Genesis 28:20-21)

He swore to return to Bethel and worship the Lord there. And he promised to give Him upon his return a tenth of all that he had, which at the time was nothing.

Jacob had been driven into the wilderness by his own sins. He was alone and afraid and ashamed of what he had done. But in the middle of nowhere, God found him. He demonstrated that the whole world was His, not just one city or shrine. And clothed in all that power and authority, He vowed to look after Jacob and to carry on the Covenant He had made with his fathers.

This encounter changed Jacob forever. "Surely the Lord is in this place, and I did not know it," he said. And he committed his whole life to Almighty God. He was still the rascal from Beersheba, but he had met God. The journey was not over, the problem was not solved, but God was with him.

HERE AND HERE

The story of Jacob's Ladder is a demonstration of the Immanence of God. To say God is immanent means that God is near; that He is available, and not out of reach. Of course, in one sense God is so far beyond us that we could never find Him on our own (Isaiah 55:9). But the Bible goes to great lengths to impress upon us the nearness of God. The Lord has not hidden Himself, but is ready to be found by those who seek Him.

The story of Jonah gives us a great lesson in the nearness of God. Jonah, son of Amittai, was what you might call a nationalist preacher. His only other recorded prophecy in the Bible comes from 2 Kings 14:25, when he predicted that God would expand Israel's borders. So when God sent him to preach to the Assyrian empire in their capital city, he balked. The Assyrians were a brutal people, and had menaced Israel for generations. The thought of offering forgiveness to his oppressors was too much for Jonah. And so, "Jonah rose to flee to Tarshish from the presence of the Lord" (Jonah 1:3).

Remember what we said before about the theology of the day. It was believed that the gods were restricted to their respective territories. The gods supposedly lost power and influence according to the distance from their temples. That's why Jonah fled to Tarshish, perhaps as far away as Spain. God would never find him there, right?

Wrong. The Lord sent a terrible storm to rock the boat until Jonah fessed up to the rest of the crew. "I am a Hebrew," he said, "and I fear the Lord, the God of heaven, who made the sea and the dry land" (Jonah 1:9). What's the point? God made the whole world, and therefore the whole world is His domain. God's mastery over nature is evident in the book of Jonah. The sea, the fish, the sun, the wind, the plant, and the worm are all under His control. As the Psalmist said,

"Where shall I go from your Spirit? Or where shall I flee from your presence?" (Psalm 139:7)

Jonah learned it on the waters, Jacob learned it at Bethel: God is near. The gateway to Heaven is not confined to a single location, because God is not bound by space. Even when Solomon built Israel's Temple, he said,

> "Behold, heaven and the heaven of heavens cannot contain you; how much less this house that I have built!" (1 Kings 8:27)

The world around you is thrumming with the presence of God. Don't mistake me. God is not "in everything," in some weird, Pantheist sense. But He is there. The immortal, invisible God is close at hand.

Not only is God there, but God is *there*. What do I mean by that? Sometimes when my wife is speaking to me, I'll zone out and fail to hear what she's saying. When she snaps her fingers to get my attention, I'll say, "I'm here!" To which she wittily replies, "Yes, but you're not *here*." Maybe your parents have said that to you when you're on your phone at the dinner table. The first sense is that of being present, literally in the room. God is "here" because He is omnipresent. But the second sense is that of being aware and engaged. God is also *here* in that sense. He knows, He cares, and He is prepared to act.

> "Am I a God at hand, declares the Lord, and not a God far away? Can a man hide himself in secret places so that I cannot see him? declares the Lord. Do I not fill heaven and earth? declares the Lord." (Jeremiah 23:23-24)

God defines Himself in opposition to the false gods of the nations by His participation in the story. There's a beautiful passage in the book of Job where He describes His attendance at the birth of baby fawns in the woods (Job 39). Let's rid ourselves of the notion of a distant God with little interest in His Creation. He cares about each individual life. See how He promised to be with Jacob through all of his wanderings until journey's end. God has given you a destiny, and He intends to see it through. "I will not leave you until I have done what I promised you," He said.

"From of old no one has heard or perceived by the ear, no eye has seen a God besides you, who acts for those who wait for him." (Isaiah 64:4)

Because God is Immanent – here and *here* – He will answer you if you call upon Him. Remember all those verses about finding God I crammed into that song before? Here's a few more:

"Seek the Lord and his strength; seek his presence continually!" (Psalm 105:4)

"You will seek me and find me, when you seek me with all your heart." (Jeremiah 29:13)

"Jesus answered him, 'If anyone loves me, he will keep my word, and my Father will love him, and we will come to him and make our home with him.'" (John 14:23)

"Behold, I stand at the door and knock. If anyone hears my voice and opens the door, I will come in to him and eat with him, and he with me." (Revelation 3:20)

God is not far from you. In fact, speaking of the nearness of God, Jesus even said, "The kingdom of God is in the midst of you" (Luke 17:21). You can know God. If you seek after God, you will find Him. Because He is there. Because He cares. And because He is already looking for you (John 12:32).

OPEN THE EYES OF MY HEART

Jacob caught a glimpse of the other side of the world. The realm, or dimension, beyond what could be observed with the senses. There's a similar story in the book of 2 Kings. The king of Syria sent an army to arrest the prophet Elisha, surrounding the city in the middle of the night. The next morning, Elisha's servant, Gehazi, panicked at the sight, but the prophet told him to calm down because the enemy was outnumbered.

"Then Elisha prayed and said, 'O Lord, please open his eyes that he may see.' So the Lord opened the eyes of the young man, and he saw, and behold, the mountain was full of horses and chariots of fire all around Elisha." (2 Kings 6:17)

The angelic army was already there, but Gehazi did not have the eyes to see it. We too must open our eyes to see what is truly there. I'm not talking about dreams and visions necessarily, but an understanding that there is more to the world than what we see. I think most of us know that instinctively. Every culture believes in spirits and ghosts and gods and magic, and most people in our culture do as well. There is a lot of foolishness surrounding this subject, but that does not minimize the reality of what the Bible teaches. Why would you believe that only the material is real? Have we not learned that life is more than matter?

"We look not to the things that are seen but to the things that are unseen. For the things that are seen are transient, but the things that are unseen are eternal." (2 Corinthians 4:18)

The world around you is staggeringly alive! The angels are there, as Jacob and Elisha saw. The fallen angels, or demons, are there too, as was revealed to Daniel and John. Most of all, the Lord is there, who fills all things. There is a whole invisible world of spiritual activity all around you. And your spirit is able to engage with that world. Therefore, you must pray, in the words of a classic worship song: "Open the eyes of my heart, Lord!"

You must encounter God in the wilderness. If you have gone into the unknown (willingly or unwillingly), if you want to fulfill your calling, then you must meet God. This is the major difference between the world with its "Hero's Journey", and the Christian experience. You must encounter God. Not symbolically, not metaphorically, but actually.

Near the end of his life, the fiery preacher Leonard Ravenhill was asked what he saw as the greatest problem in the Church today. Without hesitation, he replied, "We don't know God." He went on to describe how so many preachers know Greek and Hebrew, or know ministry techniques, but all of that was useless apart from experiential knowledge of God. That is why Jesus came. He prayed to His Father at the Last Supper,

"This is eternal life, that they know you, the only true God, and Jesus Christ whom you have sent." (John 17:3)

It is not only beneficial to know God, it is essential. To encounter His presence by the Holy Spirit. To learn His ways in the Scriptures. To carry on a conversation through prayer. To be introduced to Him by other believers. Do these things seem ordinary to you? I assure you that if you seek the Lord in this way, in worship and the Word, then you will find Him.

Most of my Christian life (and I would say this is typical) consists of regular, nothing-to-report days. Countless Sundays when the music went well, the sermon was alright, and the people were friendly. But nothing special. Then there are those days or nights when the Lord lays you out. When the same songs you've sung a thousand times suddenly hit harder than ever before, bringing you to shout for joy, or even to tears. The same preacher you've always heard suddenly speaks with a power that has nothing to do with him, and now you are shaking in your seat, or burning with a fire in your bones. Your evening prayers go from routine to revolutionary as you find yourself sprawled on the carpet, losing all track of time because you are overwhelmed with the love of God in Christ Jesus.

Have you ever had an experience like that? If you've been a Christian for any length of time, you probably have. And you probably know that these moments can be life-changing. Bad habits are overcome in an instant, broken hearts are healed without medication, wisdom and direction flow from above. That's the kind of encounter Jacob had at Bethel.

The last thing I want to do is pressure you to "make something happen." As I said, it is boring discipline that lays the foundation for the major construction. But if you seek the Lord, you will find Him. As we sing at our church sometimes, "Let us become more aware of Your presence! Let us experience the glory of Your goodness!" God is already there, but we're aching for Him to show Himself. And God delights to make Himself known.

Why? Because He loves us. God looks at you like a Father looks at His child (Psalm 103:13). I have four children, and I absolutely love being around them. Nothing is better than walking through the door and hearing little feet running to greet you with hugs and kisses. That kind of father-love comes from the Father of us all, who loves us "with an everlasting love" (Jeremiah 31:3). Why would we expect Him to hide Himself from us?

You'll never get through this alone, but there is no need to. God is invested in your situation. Remember, God is the one who placed the call upon your life. He assigned you a life to live and gave you a plan and a purpose. He also knows that you are not up to the challenge, and that you have probably been knocked about up to this point. But rather than abandon you to your fate, God wants to intervene and help you along the way. "I will instruct you and teach you in the way you should go," He says in Psalm 32:8, "I will counsel you with my eye upon you."

Once you encounter God, you will never be the same. The first and greatest of all encounters, of course, is that of salvation. But every story of your life, from major career moves to breaking a bad habit, should be marked by a definite encounter with God. And it need not be a stairway to Heaven. It can be a still, small voice as you read your Bible or sit quietly in church. But do not discount the possibility of God showing Himself in a mighty way. He loves to use moments of transition as opportunities to work out lifelong changes.

There is more to the world than what you see, and the most important part of it is God Himself. Open up your eyes, seek after Him like silver, and believe me, you will find Him. Or, I should say, He will find you!

THEY SAW THE LORD

The Bible is not a textbook. It does not lay out truths about God in a systematic manner. What it does is much more effective. In addition to passages of didactic instruction, we have beautiful poetry setting those truths to music and lyrics. There are prophetic revelations that bear those truths out in symbolic, stylized language. But most of all we have narratives that demonstrate the truth about God in vibrant, powerful stories. So while the Bible tells us plainly that God is near and ready to be found by those who seek Him (Isaiah 65:1, James 4:8), it also shows us over and over again.

Every man of God has an unforgettable encounter with the Lord that marks him for life. We've already seen a few of these: Moses at the burning bush, Paul on the road to Damascus, Jonah in the great fish, Jacob's ladder. But the examples don't stop there.

Abraham had a number of encounters with God, each one building upon the last. In Genesis 12, God simply told him to go to the Promised Land, and affirmed him when he arrived. In Genesis 15, God sent him outside to number the stars. In Genesis 17, God sent Abraham into a deep sleep and gave him a vision of His glory passing between the Covenant offering. And in Genesis 18, three men came to visit Abraham, one of whom was the Angel of the Lord Himself. This is why Abraham is known as the "friend of God" (James 2:23).

Isaiah had a memorable encounter with God. "In the year that King Uzziah died," he wrote, "I saw the Lord sitting upon a throne, high and lifted up; and the train of his robe filled

describes mighty angels worshiping the Lord with l

the foundations of the thresholds shook at the voice ᴏɪ ɪ...

and the house was filled with smoke." This caused Isaiah to despair for his life until an angel touched his lips with a burning coal from the altar (Isaiah 6:1-7). This was immediately followed by Isaiah's call as a prophet. Do you think Isaiah could ever doubt his calling after an experience like that?

The children of Israel were granted a similar experience when they first arrived at Mount Sinai. For three days Moses had the people prepare for the coming of the Lord.

> "On the morning of the third day there were thunders and lightnings and a thick cloud on the mountain and a very loud trumpet blast, so that all the people in the camp trembled...Mount Sinai was wrapped in smoke because the Lord had descended on it in fire. The smoke of it went up like the smoke of a kiln, and the whole mountain trembled greatly." (Exodus 19:16, 18)

This is when God spoke out the Ten Commandments. The people were so terrified that they asked Moses to do all the talking to God from now on! The Lord was not angry with them, though. The whole point was to let them know who they were dealing with in this Covenant they were making (Exodus 20:20).

Then Simon Peter encountered the Lord in an experience that was less dramatic, but no less wonderful. On the night of the crucifixion, Peter denied Jesus three times. Then after the Resurrection, Jesus appeared to the disciples at the Sea of Galilee. Peter was so overjoyed he jumped out of the boat and swam to the shore fully clothed. As they sat around the campfire, Jesus asked him three times, "Simon, son of John, do you love me?" And it says,

> "Peter was grieved because he said to him the third time, 'Do you love me?'" (John 21:17)

Peter knew that this was his restoration; he needed to face up to what he had done and recommit himself to the Lord. When he did, Jesus commissioned him to feed His sheep, and to follow Him. Peter would go on to lead the Church, write Scripture, and die a martyr's death.

These are varied experiences. Some of them were mighty and powerful, like the visions of Ezekiel, but others were small and personal, like the "whisper" Elijah heard on the mountain (1 Kings 19:12). Not every encounter is going to be the same. But when you encounter the Lord, you will never be the same.

THE SAME STORY

I attended a student Bible study during my time in seminary. We met at the White Hart, a dangerous-turned-trendy coffee house in Lynchburg, Virginia. After the meeting I was talking with a few of the guys, and I mentioned something that the Lord had said to me personally. One of the fellows stopped me and eagerly asked, "So you believe that you can actually hear the voice of God?" I was surprised. All that academic training, and they still had no knowledge of something so important. I gave them the same answer I give to you: If Moses could speak to God face to face (Exodus 33:11), and the Holy Spirit would give answers to the Church when they prayed and fasted

(Acts 13:2), then certainly we, who have the same Holy Spirit within us, have the same right of access to hear from God (John 16:13).

The Bible is God's ineffable Word, but it should never just be a book of stories for you. You must have your own stories that resonate with what you find in Scripture. You should be able to read about the character of God and nod your head in agreement because you have seen it for yourself. You are part of the story of the faithful. God can be to you what He was to all those Bible heroes you read about.

It can be hard to shake off the insidious Naturalism of the modern day. Even if we formally believe that there are such things as miracles, angels, and God Himself, we can hesitate at the doorway of experience. But don't let some smarty-pants with a Ph.D. rob you of your spiritual inheritance. When you define your terms by strict materialism, then you have ruled out the supernatural by default, not by empirical proof.

But I have tasted and seen that these things are true. If you seek the Lord with all your heart, you will find Him. Everyone calls themselves a seeker, but most people seek within a very narrow band of possibility. There are beliefs they will not question, roads down which they will not travel. But those who seek honestly and desperately always end up at the feet of Jesus (Matthew 7:7-8).

For it is only through Jesus Christ that we may truly know God (John 14:6). The most important way that God has opened a Gate to Heaven, so to speak, is in the person of His Son. When Nathanael acknowledged that Jesus was the Son of God, and the rightful King of Israel, Jesus was impressed at his readiness to believe.

"And he said to him, 'Truly, truly, I say to you, you will see heaven opened, and the angels of God ascending and descending on the Son of Man.'" (John 1:51)

Jesus is the ultimate self-revelation of God. And it is through His death on the cross that God has opened up the way to Heaven, as evidenced by His resurrection. It is Jesus that you must seek in the wilderness, for He is the only way to God.

Jacob was not looking for God in the wilderness. But it's what he needed. In the same way, you might only be looking for a solution to your problems, but God has bigger plans. He's beckoning you to follow Him. He knows the way through this wilderness, and He alone can sustain you along the journey. So even if you're not exactly sure what it will mean for you, it's time to humble yourself like Jacob did. You may have done it a thousand times before, but every journey, every new day, requires a fresh encounter with Jesus, and a fresh commitment to follow His lead.

"The kingdom of heaven is like treasure hidden in a field, which a man found and covered up. Then in his joy he goes and sells all that he has and buys that field." (Matthew 13:44)

There is treasure buried in the field. So go get it! Cry out into the darkness if you must. God will hear you. He will speak to you. Take a step of faith, the stakes are far too high. Because if God may be known? Nothing else matters.

STUDY QUESTIONS

1.) Why do you think Fantasy and Science Fiction entertainment is so popular in our secular culture? Is there truth underneath some of our favorite shows and books?

2.) Read again all the Bible references about seeking and finding God. How does it make you feel to know that God has invited us to know Him so many times?

3.) How does Jacob's Bethel, "House of God", compare and contrast with Babylon, "Gate of the Gods"? What was God trying to communicate with that name?

4.) Do you understand the Immanence of God? What does it mean to be both here and *here*? Is that intimidating or comforting to you?

5.) What does the Bible teach about angels and demons? How should that affect our daily lives?

6.) Would you agree with Leonard Ravenhill that the greatest goal of a Christian should be to know God? Is there anything that you would not give up to know God? Why or why not?

7.) Have you ever had an amazing encounter with God? Does the possibility of moments like that motivate you to keep coming back?

8.) Why is it significant that Isaiah saw the Lord in the year King Uzziah died (Isaiah 6)? How does Isaiah's reaction to God's presence instruct us about our own posture before Him?

9.) Do you know the voice of the Lord? Can you tell when He is speaking to you? How might you go about learning His voice?

10.) If Jesus is the supreme revelation of God, then what does that teach us about God? Would you be more likely to approach Jesus than God in Heaven? Pray and ask the Lord to reveal Himself to you in a special way.

6

THE MONSTER IN
THE MIRROR

JACOB MEETS LABAN

(Genesis 29:1-30)

THE QUEEN OF HEARTS

The villain is often the most interesting part of a great story. It seems like the bad guys have more fans, sell more t-shirts and inspire more tattoos than the heroes ever do. The most compelling villains are an inversion of the hero. They are the ultimate symbol of everything the hero is trying to overcome. Aragorn is haunted by the kings who have fallen to the temptation of the Ring: Isildur, Denethor, and of course the nine Ringwraiths. Wendy is reluctant to grow up, as are Peter Pan, the immature child, and Captain Hook, the neurotic pirate terrified of the ticking clock. One of the best examples is from Disney's version of *Alice in Wonderland*.

The movie opens with Alice wishing for a world without rules, where everything is nonsense. She tumbles down the rabbit hole into Wonderland, which is exactly that. Immediately she realizes the frustration of such an arbitrary world. As the film progresses, she grows more and more angry with the denizens of Wonderland, until she finds herself lost in the woods. Tearfully, she asks the Cheshire Cat for help, who opens a door to the grounds of a castle. Who rules in such a bizarre place as this? A short-tempered tyrant called the Queen of Hearts. She orders executions willy-nilly and barks commands to suit her varying whims. Alice is in real danger when she is brought before the Queen in a courtroom where the laws are all made up.

This is a silly movie for children, but the lesson is profound. In a world where everything is nonsense, the only rules are those that can be enforced by someone in power. Those without it live in terror, and the ones with it are at the mercy of their own caprice. A terrified Alice runs for her life to escape the dream. She has seen the end result of an idea that sounded great, but could only lead to tyranny and rage. The real world that seemed so boring is now comforting and stable.

If we could see where our ideas were leading us, we would be much more careful with our decisions. While cigarette cartons in America have warnings from the Surgeon General, other countries have pictures of blackened lungs and rotten gums. A negative view of where you are headed can be a strong motivation to change.

When we are cast into the wilderness, the first thing to do is to meet God. But the first place God will take you is deeper into the wilderness to see who you really are. He takes you to meet the Queen of Hearts. Because even when we have caused terrible damage by our own sins, we can be extremely crafty in making excuses for ourselves. We believe that our sins are manageable, or unavoidable, or even beneficial – like slaveowners before the Civil War. But God wants to show us the depths of our own depravity so that we are willing to submit to His instruction. It's not always pleasant to look in the mirror, but the consequences of looking away are far too great.

DUELING TRICKSTERS

In Genesis 29, Jacob arrived at the well in Haran. The shepherds were gathered to water the flocks, and they confirmed that Laban, Jacob's uncle, was still a resident there.

> "While he was still speaking with them, Rachel came with her father's sheep, for she was a shepherdess." (Genesis 29:8)

Immediately, Jacob was smitten! He rolled away the large stone covering the well and watered her flock. "Then Jacob kissed Rachel and wept aloud," as he explained who he was, the son of her father's sister (Genesis 29:11-12).

This picture is parallel to what happened when Rebekah was betrothed to Isaac. In Genesis 24, Abraham sent his servant to find a bride for his son. At that same well, the servant prayed for God to show him the right woman. Rebekah fulfilled his prayer by offering him a drink and watering his camels for him. Jacob seems to be re-living his parents' romance, exactly as they had hoped.

Upon their meeting, Laban welcomed Jacob into the family, another seeming success. Now, the last time we saw Laban, he spoke well to Abraham's servant, but tried to delay Rebekah's return. We get the sense from that story that Laban was trying to weasel a little more of Abraham's wealth away before they left. It doesn't take long for money to come up in this story either.

After a month, "Laban said to Jacob, 'Because you are my kinsman, should you therefore serve me for nothing? Tell me, what shall your wages be?'" (Genesis 29:15)

This seems generous at first, unless you have had the unfortunate experience of introducing money into a family relationship. But Jacob was not interested in money. He wanted to marry Laban's daughter. "Rachel was beautiful in form and appearance," and so Jacob offered to serve Laban for seven years as a bride price. He had no money, so his labor was the only thing he could offer. Laban agreed, and Jacob spent seven years in Haran,

"And they seemed to him but a few days because of the love he had for her." (Genesis 29:20)

Well, isn't that sweet!

Finally, the big day came, and Jacob asked for the wedding to be held at once. "Laban gathered together all the people of the place and made a feast" (Genesis 29:22). Surely Jacob rejoiced that God had given him exactly what he came for. But then everything went terribly, terribly wrong.

You see, Laban had two daughters. Rachel was the youngest, and she was beautiful, as we have seen. The other's name was Leah, and it says her "eyes were weak" (Genesis 29:17). It's not exactly certain what this means. It could be that she had different color eyes than was usual in this culture (perhaps blue?), it could be that she had poor eyesight. But because it is said in contrast to Rachel's beauty, it is entirely possible that this is a Hebrew euphemism meaning something like, "Hard on the Eyes"! Whatever the case, it is clear that Rachel is the desirable one, while Leah seems to be having trouble finding a husband.

And so Laban did something on Jacob's wedding night that just might be the most despicable thing you or I have ever heard of:

> "In the evening, he took his daughter Leah and brought her to Jacob, and he went in to her...And in the morning, behold, it was Leah!" (Genesis 29:23, 25)

Laban deliberately married Jacob to the wrong woman, and he did not realize it until the next morning, after their wedding night!

How is this possible? The bride would have worn a veil for the ceremony, and it was likely very dark by the time the feast was over. But the best explanation is that Jacob was quite drunk after the great feast, no doubt helped along by Laban's encouragement. And when he woke up, he realized he had consummated his marriage with his fiancée's sister.

The Bible does not give us many details about what happened next, but I can imagine Jacob's startled cry rang out through the city of Haran. He marched down to his father-in-law and had a very *loud* discussion.

> "What is this you have done to me?" he demanded, "Why have you deceived me?" (Genesis 29:25)

Laban put him off by insisting that local custom demanded the eldest daughter be married first, and then offered Jacob the chance to marry Rachel as well – for another seven years of servitude.

The fox had been outfoxed. The trickster had been tricked. The Heel-Catcher's heel had been caught. Jacob experienced a shame even greater than that which he had brought upon his father. He agreed to marry Rachel, which he did after only a week, and began another seven years of employment to Laban. But now he has two literal sister-wives, and whatever trust he had in his father-in-law (or wives, I might add) is broken.

Jacob thought he was sneaky, but Laban was the ultimate sneak, the consummate deceiver. He was the worst version of Jacob's worst tendencies. And Jacob got a chance to look in the mirror and see who he would become if he continued down the road he was travelling.

SURPRISING SELF-DECEPTION

One of the oddest things about us as people is that we have the ability to lie to ourselves. In fact, we have the ability to lie to ourselves *about* ourselves. And the most common lie we tell ourselves is that we have our vices under control. Gambling addicts do this all the time: "I've got it all figured out! I can beat the odds! I can stop any time I want to!" But whether it's gambling or greed or gossip, we all know deep down that we're just stalling for time.

We have already taken an honest look at the mess of our lives, and daydreamed with God about how they might be better. This step is related to that one, but much more painful. You must face up to the fact that you are the problem, and that your shortcomings have contributed to the mess you are in. Yes, there may be other people who have hurt you, and perhaps you were never taught what is right. But the way forward begins with admitting your own complicity in the evils of the world. Jacob was a liar and a trickster, so God brought him to an unscrupulous con-artist to show him what he really was.

Have you ever surprised yourself? That's another thing we can do that doesn't make a lot of sense. I remember one time when I was in high school, I was driving down the road, talking to my mom on speaker phone. She got another call and put me on hold. While I was waiting, another driver cut me off on Old Graves Mill Rd. and I almost crashed the car. Immediately I let loose with an impressive string of loud curses and imprecations, pounding the steering wheel at the reckless driver in front of me.

Then I remembered I was still on speaker phone with my mother!

"...Mom?" I asked tentatively.

A few seconds went by, and then the phone clicked.

"Okay, I'm back!" she said cheerfully.

She had heard none of my shouted profanity. I've never been so relieved in my life. Cursing was out of character for me, even then. That outburst in the car surprised me, and revealed a few things I was harboring without realizing it.

When we surprise ourselves like that, it shows us that there are things inside that we have not dealt with yet. Jesus said in Matthew 12:34, "Out of the abundance of the heart the mouth speaks." Those words would not have come out of me if they were not already in me. When you suddenly become violent to someone you love, or give your number to a man that is not your husband, or steal from the register at work, that is a warning of what's really going on in your heart.

This is not to say that you do not know, in your head, what is right. Or that you would defend your worst tendencies. To the contrary, it is often the most religious who break bad the hardest. They think they are beyond petty little sins until they are pushed to a place they weren't ready to go.

This is why James warns us,

"Be doers of the word, and not hearers only, deceiving yourselves. For if anyone is a hearer of the word and not a doer, he is like a man who looks intently at his natural face in a mirror. For he looks at himself and goes away and at once forgets what he was like. But the one who looks into the perfect law, the law of liberty, and perseveres, being no hearer who forgets but a doer who acts, he will be blessed in his doing." (James 1:22-25)

James was the brother of Jesus. Like his Brother, he grew up in the rough town of Nazareth (John 1:46), as a construction worker (Mark 6:3). James had little patience with Jesus' Messianic pretensions (as he saw them). The Gospel of John records a rough falling out between Jesus and his brothers before the Feast of Tabernacles, when they taunted Him for a coward and a fraud. It says, "For not even his brothers believed in him" (John 7:5). But after the Resurrection, Jesus appeared specifically to James (1 Corinthians 15:7), and on the day of Pentecost, the skeptical brother was there (Acts 1:14). He went on to become the pastor of the church in Jerusalem. Paul would call him a "pillar" (Galatians 2:9). Church history tells us that he was known for his compassion and his prayer, but his epistle shows that he never lost that blue-collar impatience with hypocrisy.

He tells us that we must be doers of the Word of God, not just hearers. Those who know what is right but don't apply it he compares to those who look in a mirror and then forget what they see. The point of looking in a mirror is to see yourself. How's my hair? Do I need a shave? Is my tie straight? But if you see a piece of cilantro stuck in your teeth and walk away without removing it, what good did looking in the mirror do you? It's the same thing with knowing the truth about yourself. If you know you have a temper, or homosexual attraction, or a tendency to lie, but you never do anything about it, then of what value to you is knowing the truth?

That is why God wants to take us into the depths of ourselves, to show us how bad the problem really is. Have you ever had a toothache that you ignored until you needed a root canal? Jacob knew he was a bit of a sneak, but he needed to realize just how dangerous that attitude was. The betrayal of his family was not an isolated incident. His deception would continue to hurt the ones he loved until he was willing to renounce his status as the Heel-Catcher. He needed to take a look in the mirror.

And there is no better way to do that than to see your own trajectory played out in someone else's life. That's why they put those gross images on packs of cigarettes. That's why we share testimonies in church. And that's why God gave us the Scriptures, so that we could see wisdom and folly played out to the end. But there's nothing as memorable as being hurt by somebody who acts just like you. That is why God sent Jacob to Laban.

One of my favorite books is the classic *Heart of Darkness*. It's a short novella about a sophisticated Englishman who turns vicious in the heart of the Congo jungle. He believed himself to be superior to the savage peoples of the dark continent, but in the wilderness he found himself to be equally ferocious. On his deathbed, he considers all that he has done and gasps out, "The horror! The horror!"

The world will tell you to trust your heart. But God knows that,

"The heart is deceitful above all things, and desperately sick; who can understand it?" (Jeremiah 17:9)

You have a heart of darkness. But one hard look in the mirror can be just the thing to snap you out of your nonchalance.

SOWING AND REAPING

You might not think that your little vices are such a big deal. You look at the failures of other people and never consider that it could happen to you. But Jesus compared us to crops in a field.

> "You will recognize them by their fruits. Are grapes gathered from thornbushes, or figs from thistles?" (Matthew 7:16)

Whatever seeds you plant in your heart are going to germinate and grow. There's a scene in *Secondhand Lions* where the men notice that something is wrong with their garden. They realize that everything they planted looks the same. Turns out the traveling salesman had sold them packets of seeds with nothing but corn. To their embarrassment and frustration, instead of a vibrant garden, they end up with a massive cornfield. You likewise need to know what it is you're planting.

> "Do not be deceived: God is not mocked, for whatever one sows, that will he also reap. For the one who sows to his own flesh will from the flesh reap corruption, but the one who sows to the Spirit will from the Spirit reap eternal life." (Galatians 6:7-8)

Lucky for you and me, we are not the first men to live on the earth. We have the benefit of thousands of years of hindsight and reflection, not to mention the testimony of the Bible. Most every moral decision has been tried at some point, and the results are in. There are plenty of examples for us to look to. The seed packets have little pictures on the front so you can know what you're getting.

What about sexual immorality? Most of us have dabbled in it, all the while swearing that we will never cross "that" line. But lust always breaks the levee. What begins with an improper gaze can lead to a shameful act or a disgraceful failure (Matthew 5:27-28). How many people view their pornography addiction as a harmless thing? But it trains your mind and feeds your lust. "Oh, we're not going to have sex, we're just going to sleep in the same bed." Yeah, right. Marriages, careers and nations have fallen apart because of sexual immorality, don't mess with it.

What about pride? We all struggle with pride – especially those of us who don't think we do. Pride can be arrogance, swaggering, boasting, and picking fights. But pride can also be introverted, judgmental and smug. Your little comments about how stupid everyone else is, or how lame, or how lazy, are expressions of your ego. Pride unchecked will drive everyone from you and blow up your relationships (Proverbs 16:18). And yet you'll still be standing there, empty and alone, thinking you were in the right all the time.

What about gluttony? Yes, America, gluttony is still a sin (Philippians 3:19). We of all people should know this. Overindulgence in food is not just a bad idea, it is wicked. The consequences of this one are easy to see, because they literally grow on you. If you find yourself compulsively driving-thru, finishing off everyone's leftovers, and sneaking out of bed for more, you've got a problem. There is no realm of sin with more excuses than gluttony. But you are mistreating the body God gave you, hurting the people you love, and limiting the enjoyment of your own life by refusing to tell yourself, "No".

Closely related, what about sloth? Living lazy is not a personality type, it is a sin. You are acting as though your life is not worth living, or that your life is everyone else's responsibility. The Bible tells us not to love sleep (Proverbs 20:13), but to rise and get to work. Proverbs in particular overflows with warnings about the danger that comes from failing to work hard (Proverbs 6:10-11). You end up broke, desperate and stuck. And that's an open door for all kinds of bitterness.

Anger is an easy one. But some of us have found a way to excuse our bad temper. "It's just the way I was raised. It's part of my culture. It's my way of protecting my family." It all amounts to a lack of self-control (Ephesians 4:26). Maybe your anger is exclusively online, or just with certain people. Unchecked anger leads to violence, vile language, and even murder, Jesus said (Matthew 5:21-22). Don't wave it off, deal with it now.

What about lying? The Bible says the truth will set you free (John 8:32), that God is the God of truth (Psalm 31:5), and that He hates everyone who loves and practices a lie (Revelation 22:15). The Devil is called the father of lies (John 8:44). God insists that we face the world as it is, and that we represent the truth without error. Little lies are not excusable, even if they are made to the corrupt or rich or powerful. You've seen lies undo a person's friendships, finances, even their freedom. Stop indulging the little lies that have taken root in your life.

And what about greed? The desire to have what is not yours, covetousness, avarice, all of that. Greed is more than just a desire to have more, it is the determined refusal to enjoy life. It is the quest for status and power and possessions; an incredibly empty way to live (1 John 2:16). How many celebrities have denounced the famous life as meaningless in the end? How many filthy rich bankers have been caught trying to squeeze just a little more out of the system? The Bible says to be content with your little, or with your lot (1 Timothy 6:8). Failing to be thankful for what you have now will poison anything you might gain later on.

You might say I'm exaggerating. That I'm using the worst possible examples to scare you. That's exactly what I'm doing. It's what God was doing by bringing Jacob to see Laban. Sin is monstrous, and it turns us into monsters. You might see your sin as wrong, but not disastrous. Annoying, sure. Sub-optimal, maybe. But monstrous? Yes. Whatever benefit you expect from your sin will break your heart in the end. It happens every time. Check the label, and make sure you know what you're planting.

MEETING THE MONSTER

The heroes of the Bible are defined by how they handle the confrontation with sin. When their actions expose them for who they really are, they either humble themselves, or they double down. That decision comes to define them.

Consider what happened the night of Christ's crucifixion. Judas Iscariot, one of the Twelve disciples, had made arrangements to betray Jesus to the religious rulers. After the Passover dinner, he snuck out to fetch a band of men to arrest Him. At that same dinner, Peter swore that he would never abandon Jesus, even if everyone else did. That night in the Garden of Gethsemane, Judas betrayed Jesus to the soldiers with a kiss, and Peter ran away to save his own skin. Later that night he would deny that he even knew who Jesus was, three times.

These are two very similar situations. But the men reacted very differently. When Judas's conscience caught up with him, he tried to return the money, but it was too late. Overcome, "he went and hanged himself" (Matthew 27:5). When Peter met Jesus' eyes after his third

125

denial, as the rooster crowed, "he went out and wept bitterly" (Luke 22:62). Both were broken when they realized what they had done. Judas chose to end his own life rather than walk the hard road of repentance. But Peter would return to the other Apostles, and later see the risen Lord, who would restore him to his place among the faithful. Peter was willing to face who he was and make a change.

As the Lord told Cain when he was enraged at his brother Abel,

"Sin is crouching at the door. Its desire is contrary to you, but you must rule over it." (Genesis 4:7)

God warned him that his anger was out of control. But Cain blew it off and committed the first murder. Likewise, King Saul, when confronted with his disobedience to the Lord, did not repent or apologize. He just wanted to make sure that the prophet Samuel would keep up appearances so that the people would still listen to him (1 Samuel 15:30). Saul lost the kingdom for it.

It was given instead to David. David was not a perfect man. He committed a terrible sin by sleeping with his friend's wife and getting her pregnant. He then had Uriah killed rather than let it be known what he had done. But the prophet Nathan confronted him by telling David a story. He asked what ought to be done to punish a rich man who had stolen his neighbor's pet lamb and served it to his guest for dinner. David was outraged and demanded the man be killed. Nathan then pointed his finger at him and said, "You are the man!" (2 Samuel 12:7). He showed David the monster in the mirror by withholding the identity of the monster. When he realized what he had done, David repented in the most beautiful, heartbreaking song of regret ever written: Psalm 51. And for that reason, God forgave him.

Similarly Paul, when he realized he had been persecuting the Lord's Church, changed his entire life, even his name, to serve the Lord. That is what each of us must do. When we see the road down which we are headed, we must immediately stop and turn around. That's what it means to repent. Don't just acknowledge the problem, renounce the problem.

If not, you'll end up like Jonah. Jonah's hate led him to the stormy seas, where he was swallowed by a great fish. There's a picture for you. The monster of prejudice swallowed him up and carried him to the utter depths. And even when Jonah was set free and went to Nineveh, it became clear that he was still a prejudiced man. He was walking under the sun, yet in a very real sense he was still in the belly of the whale. He had been to the depths of his own soul, met the monster, and yet refused to change. Will you be so foolish as to persist in your own monstrosities?

"HE'S GONNA GET BIGGER!"

Pretty much every baby animal is cute. Even little rats and alligators can make the girls *Ooh* and *Aww*. But I have a hard time seeing a baby varmint as anything other than a varmint. Baby raccoons are adorable, but in about five minutes they'll be all grown up, knocking over my trash cans. That young chimpanzee will someday get sick of looking at you and rip your face off. Oh sure, the little lion has soft, downy fur. But in the words of Timon the meerkat, "He's gonna get bigger!" Get bigger, and probably eat somebody.

It's the same thing with sin. We wink at it and joke about it when it's small and we feel like we've got it under control. Parents do this with their children. When little girls are sassy, it's kind of cute. Not so much when she's 25 and can't maintain a relationship. Lots of dads are proud of their aggressive little boy. But if you don't get a handle on that, you'll be waving at that little boy through glass, talking with a little telephone on the wall.

Jacob had broken his family. His deception and passive aggression had ruined whatever love remained between them. But given time, he might have started to feel sorry for himself. He might have blamed his mother, or his father, or his brother, or even God. His own role in that scene would have shrunk to insignificance. The sin would have only grown in his heart until he hurt someone else. God loved him too much to let that happen. So He introduced Jacob to Laban, who did to him exactly what he had done to his father. Even worse than that, if you ask me. God wanted Jacob to get a good look at the monster lurking in the mirror. He could not continue life as the Heel-Catcher; something needed to change. It was through this encounter with another trickster that God would finally bring him to the place where He could make that change.

Your situation might not be all your fault, but you need to acknowledge your role in it. Where might you have been brave and spoken up to stop it? Where did you boil over and say something foolish? How did your mismanagement of money contribute to your financial collapse? It's time to see where your current path will lead you and turn around to walk the other way.

I once had a friend in my Physics class who was telling me about her new boyfriend. She knew it wasn't going to last because he was a jerk, but she figured she'd have fun while it lasted. I was baffled and asked why she'd continue a relationship that she knew was trouble. Why not break up now and find somebody who was good for her? I'll never forget her response: "I've got to make my own mistakes."

No you don't! You can let someone else make the mistakes for you. Let Jacob and David and Paul make the mistakes for you. Let history and testimony make the mistakes for you. Let the people you love that have lived longer than you warn you from going down the same path. You are not as special as you think, and that's to your benefit, because there are others around you who have fought this monster before. He can be beaten, but first you need to look him dead in the eye.

STUDY QUESTIONS

1.) What do the villains of a story teach us about the hero and the theme? Which villains illustrate this best? How do negative examples help us?

2.) Have you ever found yourself going too far? If you could have seen yourself ahead of time, would you have gone down that road?

3.) What shocks you the most about Laban's deception of Jacob? How does Laban's trickery parallel Jacob's trickery of Isaac? How is Laban a reflection of Jacob's own heart?

4.) How is the Bible a mirror for the soul? Why is it self-deception to read the Bible but not obey it? Where have you been ignoring the Word?

5.) Have you ever done something that shocked you? Did this change the way you think about yourself?

6.) Which of these sins is a temptation for you: sexual immorality, pride, gluttony, sloth, anger, lying, greed? How have you tried to justify these sins in the past, and why are they false justifications?

7.) How did Judas and Peter handle their betrayal of Jesus differently? How do you react when you see the worst side of yourself?

8.) Read Psalm 51. Knowing the background of this story (2 Samuel 11-12), does that make it more impactful? Do you need to take this attitude with your own sin?

9.) Are there any baby sins that you have been ignoring? What could that vice look like when it's "all grown up"? Is that something you want for yourself?

10.) Can you see how your own failures have contributed to the mess of your life? What negative examples can you see to help you stay away?

7

FIGHT THE
RIGHT WAY

LABAN VERSUS JACOB

(Genesis 30:25-43)

MEET THE NEW BOSS

Hopefully you did your 9th Grade homework and read *Animal Farm* by George Orwell. It's an allegory about the Soviet Union played out in a barnyard. The pigs lead the animals in revolt against their farmer and establish an animal's paradise. But as the book progresses, the pigs make small compromises that make them more like humans and less like animals. In the end, they reinstitute all the things they had risen up against in the first place.

Revolutions have a tendency to produce some of the most unstable governments in the world. If a country experiences a military coup, the likelihood of it happening again remains very high. And even though most revolutions are fought for noble causes like freedom, equality or food, the system erected afterward is often even more tyrannical than the one that came before it. Consider the French Revolution or the People's Republic of China. They crush dissent, they stifle the economy, people grow angry, and the cycle begins anew.

The tragic irony is that the revolutionaries are often no different than the leaders they intend to dethrone. They have no problem with their methods, only with the application of those methods. Executions and terrorism are not wrong, they are just aimed at the wrong people. Political violence is to be encouraged when their side is down, but suppressed when they are on top. In the words of Gavroche from the musical *Les Miserables,*

> "There was a time we killed the king
>   We tried to change the world too fast
> Now we've got another king
>   He's no better than the last"

Or, if you prefer, from The Who:

> "Meet the new boss
>   Same as the old boss"

How we fight the battle matters. If you try to overcome your faults and failures in your own strength, you will only end up maximizing those same faults and failures. If you try to get out of a lie by lying, then you have only made yourself a greater liar. Try to handle your frustrations at work by drinking, and you hamstring your ability to deal with stress. The cause may be noble, but flesh is flesh, and Satan doesn't much care which vice is dominant in your life.

When we come face to face with the monster in our mirror, we know we need to make a change. But the battle is too tough. You can't win, because the fight is with yourself. As Jacob will learn, it is only through self-renunciation and death that victory can be won. Unfortunately, he'll have to spin his wheels for a long time before he realizes that. But you and I have the opportunity to learn that lesson now, rather than becoming just like the monster in our attempts to defeat it.

DIRTY, SNEAKY THIEVES

After marrying both Rachel and Leah (and taking on two more concubines), Jacob had twelve children: eleven sons and a daughter. But for the purposes of our study, I'd like to move on to Genesis 30:25,

> "As soon as Rachel had borne Joseph, Jacob said to Laban, 'Send me away, that I may go to my own home and country.'"

At this point, Jacob had worked for Laban for fourteen years. That's seven years for Rachel, and seven for Leah. His contract was up. No doubt he was sick of living with his snake of an uncle. And so he announced his intention to depart.

But Laban was not willing to lose this pushover from whom he had already wrung so many years of service. He insisted that Jacob stay and work for him. "Name your wages, and I will give it," he said (Genesis 30:28). You or I might have chosen to tell Laban just what he could do with that job after all he had done, but instead Jacob chose to engage.

He explained that he was frustrated with living on Laban's largesse, and wanted to start earning for himself. Laban told him again to name his price, and Jacob replied,

> "Let me pass through all your flock today, removing from it every speckled and spotted sheep and every black lamb, and the spotted and speckled among the goats, and they shall be my wages." (Genesis 30:32)

That seems fair. Jacob would take the undesirable irregular breeds and leave his uncle with purebred flocks. Laban agreed.

> "But that day Laban removed the male goats that were striped and spotted, and all the female goats that were speckled and spotted, every one that had white on it, and every lamb that was black, and put them in the charge of his sons. And he set a distance of three days' journey between himself and Jacob, and Jacob pastured the rest of Laban's flock." (Genesis 30:35-36)

Can you believe this guy? Before Jacob could make it to the flocks, he gave his sons all the spotted and speckled animals and removed them three-days' distance. Leaving Jacob, once again, with nothing! Now Jacob is obligated to pasture Laban's flocks, with a starting wage of zero. Laban has managed to keep Jacob under his thumb, with no recourse other than his continued good will.

But Jacob, you remember, was a dirty, sneaky thief. Laban might have been dirtier, sneakier and thief-ier, but Jacob was no slouch in the deception game himself. Now in charge of Laban's sheep and goats, he began to selectively breed them to his own benefit.

There is an odd superstition in this passage, where Jacob peeled sticks into white stripes and placed them before the breeding sheep (Genesis 30:37-39). This was of course a pre-scientific method, and in the next chapter God will reveal that it was He who blessed the breeding of the sheep, not the sticks. But in any case, Jacob is actively seeking to breed speckled and spotted lambs for himself. He would keep his own droves separate and breed his abnormal flocks with the strongest of Laban's. The result was that all of the strongest sheep and goats were born black or spotted, and the feeble ones were solid-colored.

Jacob figured that if Laban was going to leave him unsupervised to maintain his hold over him, then he was going to take advantage of him. You can't really blame Jacob here. He hasn't been paid anything other than the wives he has married, and Laban has not exactly made a happy home for them. I can sympathize with feeling stuck. When you know you could do better, but are being held back by a boss or a parent, it eats away at you.

And so Jacob began to catch the heel of Laban.

"Thus the man increased greatly and had large flocks, female servants and male servants, and camels and donkeys." (Genesis 30:43)

Wealth was measured in livestock at this time, and Jacob leveraged it to make a rich man of himself. No doubt this infuriated Laban. We will read later that Laban switched Jacob's wages ten times in order to try and get the best of the breeding for himself.

But you will notice that God is absent from this story. Jacob is not seeking the Lord, not that we can see. And Laban is *definitely* not seeking the Lord. What we have here are two manipulative men in a duel of deception. Jacob is trying to defeat Laban, but he is playing Laban's game. Even if he were to end up winning this contest, he would end up as exactly the kind of man he was trying to defeat. He was still the Heel-Catcher.

God had brought Jacob to Laban to show him what he would become if he continued on his path of deceit and trickery. You would think that the first betrayal would have taught him his lesson, but he still had trouble dealing forthrightly. He's mealy-mouthed with Laban, asking politely for a paycheck. Then rather than confronting the situation (or leaving!), he sneaks around again to get what he wants. Nothing had changed in him. This battle was only going to bring out the worst in Jacob. But God was willing to let him struggle until he'd had enough.

IN THE FLESH?

The epistle to the Galatians was probably Paul's first, making it our best example of a young Paul's preaching. As you can imagine, this former zealous persecutor of the Church was an equally zealous defender of the Gospel after his conversion. While his letters were never easy reading, this is Paul at his most intense. He says things like, "O foolish Galatians!" (Galatians 3:1), and of those who preach another Gospel, "Let him be accursed" (Galatians 1:9).

Paul penned this letter to warn the first churches he had planted with Barnabas. A false teaching was on the move that compelled Gentile Christians to be circumcised and observe the Law of Moses in order to be saved. The apostle cannot comprehend how anyone could fall for such an obvious falsehood:

"Are you so foolish? Having begun by the Spirit, are you now being perfected by the flesh?" (Galatians 3:3)

How could they think that they needed to complete their salvation with a ritual when the Holy Spirit Himself had already sealed and saved them? Was the cross not enough?

This was the same struggle Jacob faced with Laban. He was striving in his flesh. He had met God at Bethel and sworn to serve Him, while God had promised to protect him and bless him no matter what. It was a spiritual beginning. But when Jacob arrived, he did not walk in the Spirit. When Abraham's servant came to Haran he began in prayer and had enough discernment to see through Laban's tricks. But Jacob was thinking with his flesh. He wanted Rachel and allowed himself to be suckered into a terrible contract in order to have her. He then acted in the flesh again on his wedding night and couldn't even recognize his bride. And when his uncle ripped him off yet again, he did not seek the Lord's help, but dug into his bag of tricks. It was his flesh, the same wickedness that had sent him to Haran in the first place. Paul might have asked him the same question: "Having begun by the Spirit, are you now being perfected by the flesh?"

Let's examine that word, "flesh". This is the Greek word *sarx*, which simply refers to the physical body. The Latin word is "carne", from which we derive, "carnal". If you speak Spanish, you probably recognize that word, meaning, "meat". The definition itself is not that confusing, but the theological meaning behind it is profound.

In one important sense, the flesh is a neutral term. It is not sinful to be in the body. It's never good to portray the body as wicked, because God made the body even before the Fall. Jesus Christ Himself would be made "Incarnate," that is, "In-Flesh". Often in Scripture, to

139

be "in the flesh" means only to be in the body, as opposed to a spiritual state, like that of an angel.

But then again, Romans 8:8 says,

"Those who are in the flesh cannot please God."

The primary sense of the word *sarx* in the New Testament is to refer to sin. The "flesh" is contrasted with the Spirit, or righteousness. Why use a description of the body to describe sin? Because the body has been corrupted by sin. And now the flesh has become representative of inordinate desire, natural urges taken to evil extremes. It means to be human as opposed to godly, and to serve your own impulses rather than the higher life of the spirit. Paul would describe those whose "god is their belly, and...glory in their shame, with minds set on earthly things" (Philippians 3:19). That is what it means to walk in the flesh.

It's like an old cartoon when Bugs Bunny or Donald Duck accidentally pushes the lever in a factory too far. Everything speeds up, overheats, and explodes. That's what happens to our natural desires, our flesh, under sin. Good things are bloated to the point of wickedness.

For example, the desire to sleep is a good, natural thing. But sleeping to excess is called sloth, it is fleshly. The desire to eat is a good, natural thing. But eating to excess is called gluttony, it is fleshly. The desire for sexual intercourse is a good, natural thing. But sex taken to excess has all manner of undesirable labels. To be sexually immoral is to be fleshly.

So let us return to Paul's admonition from Galatians 3:3, "Having begun by the Spirit, are you now being perfected by the flesh?" If you have begun this journey with the Lord, allowing Him to lead you through the wilderness, you are walking in the Spirit. He then reveals to you the problem areas of your life that must be corrected. You must not then make the mistake of trying to use carnal methods to overcome sin.

The ends do not justify the means in God's economy. It does not matter how holy is the battle; how we fight matters. Too many Christians care very deeply about the state of their church, but have no use for what their pastor is actually preaching. They bring their business acumen to bear on the board or their chosen ministry, because "getting it done" is the most important thing. But it's not. Such people can poison the joy of a church. Or perhaps a talented musician can move people to tears by his voice. But he sees nothing wrong with taking his pick of the women in the congregation, as long as the services stay hot. Such violations of a church's trust can do irreparable damage.

We see the problem, and agree that something must be done. But sometimes we try to have it both ways. We want to fix the issue without changing ourselves. It is for this reason that most of us end up staying in Haran for so long. Until we have seen how deadly the flesh really is, we will remain trapped by it.

> "For the desires of the flesh are against the Spirit, and the desires of the Spirit are against the flesh, for these are opposed to each other, to keep you from doing the things you want to do." (Galatians 5:17)

Your corrupt, sinful tendencies are exactly what are keeping you from real transformation. Don't look to them for help.

"I'VE TRIED EVERY RELIGION!"

I had a friend working on the junk truck. He was a funny guy, a bit of a braggart, and willing to talk about absolutely anything. He had no issues with me as a pastor or a Christian, he just insisted that faith was not for him.

"I've tried every religion." he once pronounced confidently.

"What?" I laughed.

"I've tried every religion," he repeated, "and it's all nonsense" (he didn't actually say "nonsense", but this is a Christian book).

"You haven't tried every religion," I scoffed.

"Yes I have," he insisted.

He told me his story. To be fair, my friend had dabbled in an impressive array of denominations, religions and cults. He had been a Muslim, a Mormon, a Jehovah's Witness, a Baptist, a Catholic, and more. But something was missing.

"You haven't tried Jesus," I said.

"I just told you I went to church!" he shot back.

"Yeah," I said, "but you told me yesterday that you were sleeping with the pastor's daughter and selling drugs to the folks in the choir. You might have gone to church, but you didn't try Christianity, and you certainly didn't try Jesus!"

"Alright," he laughed, "alright."

That's kind of a funny story, but don't miss the important point. You can be engaged in all kinds of activity that looks very religious or moral or meaningful, but if you are walking in the flesh, you are just spinning your wheels. Jacob was in a dramatic back-and-forth with his uncle. It was a breathless story to watch, but he wasn't getting anywhere.

I don't know why you're reading this book. It could be that you've reached a serious turning point in your life. Or something as simple as trying to overcome an unwanted habit. Whatever the case, you have probably tried a few things to handle your problem before this. And if you're like me, you have been discouraged that nothing seems to work. That is because to fight flesh with flesh is a losing battle.

Let's look at a few of the most common ways that we strive in the flesh. None of these are evil in and of themselves. They are great helps that you ought to incorporate into your life. But if you try to solve spiritual problems with these tactics alone, you will only end up further frustrated.

The first one is willpower. We determine to resist every temptation and white-knuckle our way to freedom. Willpower is important, but by itself it is of little use in overcoming your spiritual struggles. Swearing off weed is just talking if you don't address the reason why you get high in the first place. And if your source of motivation is your own will, then what happens when what you really want at the moment is a hit? Commitments are great, but they are as easy to break as they are to make.

Second is the intellect. We convince ourselves through diligent study and argumentation that our vices are unsustainable. It's good to be smart. But smart people have a bad habit of saying one thing and doing another. It might be logical to save your money, keep a budget and invest carefully, but how do you handle the sudden impulse to upgrade your car? You can logic yourself into all sorts of foolishness. How many broke people have degrees in finance? How many countries and businesses with financial eggheads on retainer are totally bankrupt? Life is not just about knowing what is right; that's not even half the battle.

Related to that is number three: organization. This can range from a daily planner to an entirely new social structure. Anything that believes a perfect system will ensure optimal performance. We ought to have good systems, and organization is certainly a virtue. But systems are made up of people, even a system of one. And people do not always fit well into organizational structures. Lots of people have systems that promise to eliminate poverty forever. But they only seem to work by killing off anyone who doesn't agree with the system. Trust me, I have tried more personal organization schemes than anybody else I know. And I have learned over the decades that the system is not the problem.

Hard work is number four. We promise ourselves that we will do whatever is necessary to get it done. Work as many hours, do as many push-ups, pray as many times as it takes to overcome the flesh. I'm a big fan of hard work, as is the Lord. But you can work your whole life toward fixing yourself and wind up no better than the day you started. Fresh efforts to read the Bible or pray or tithe have a tendency to crash and burn. Then we feel worse, and doubt whether we'll ever get out of this mess. Or if we do succeed, we get so prideful that we've got a whole different problem to solve. You ought to work hard on your life, but that can't be the only thing.

Finally, number five is passion. In order to overcome sin or bad habits or scary circumstances, we try to work up our emotions. We figure if we can get angry enough, or excited enough, we'll be able to push through and make our way out. Nothing wrong with passion. In fact, the Bible tells us not to be lazy in our zeal (Romans 12:11). But it's unsustainable. If you try to fix your marriage by constantly seeking higher and higher romantic moments, you will exhaust yourself. How many altar calls to rededicate your life do you need? Passion is a poor foundation for a life well-lived.

This might feel like a real cynical chapter, but you need to hear this. All these methods will wear you out and get you nowhere. You might even end up angry at God for your many failures. But all of these are striving according to the flesh. That's not how God taught us to do it.

> "For I know that nothing good dwells in me, that is, in my flesh. For I have the desire to do what is right, but not the ability to carry it out." (Romans 7:18)

You ever feel that way? It's time to stop striving.

THE RIGHT THING THE WRONG WAY

When we try to achieve a spiritual goal in a fleshly way, we will not succeed. This is still true when the goal we are chasing is important, even God's will. Many people in the Bible had to learn this lesson the hard way.

While the children of Israel were wandering in the wilderness, they grew thirsty and complained to Moses. It had been decades since they were denied entry to the Promised Land, and Moses was understandably frazzled. Here they are, crying out for water, when God had clearly demonstrated His ability to miraculously provide for their needs. In Exodus 17, God had given water from a rock when Moses struck it with his staff. And so,

> "Moses and Aaron gathered the assembly together before the rock, and he said to them, 'Hear now, you rebels: shall we bring water for you out of this rock?' And Moses lifted up his hand and struck the

145

rock with his staff twice, and water came out abundantly, and the congregation drank, and their livestock." (Numbers 20:10-11)

But there was a problem. God had told Moses in Numbers 20:8 to speak to the rock, only. Instead, Moses had called the people rebels, and cracked his staff against the rock in a fit of anger. The Lord was not pleased. He said,

> "Because you did not believe in me, to uphold me as holy in the eyes of the people of Israel, therefore you shall not bring this assembly into the land that I have given them." (Numbers 20:12)

Moses was kept out of the Promised Land because he had led God's people in the flesh and so misrepresented God's mercy and patience.

Here's another example. During the tenure of Eli the high priest, the Ark of the Covenant was stolen by the Philistines. When God afflicted them with plagues, they put the Ark on a cart and sent it back to Israel. The Ark was placed at the house of a man named Abinadab, instead of the Tabernacle. So when David established himself as king in Jerusalem, he sent for the Ark. It was a time of great rejoicing, with the Ark placed on a cart driven by Abinadab's sons. But,

> "When they came to the threshing floor of Nacon, Uzzah put out his hand to the ark of God and took hold of it, for the oxen stumbled. And the anger of the Lord was kindled against Uzzah, and God struck him down there because of his error, and he died there beside the ark of God." (2 Samuel 6:6-7)

The Ark of the Covenant belonged in the Tabernacle, and it belonged in Jerusalem. But the Lord had given Israel a prescribed method of transporting it. Instead of being carried by the priests upon long poles under a blue covering, it was thrown into the back of a cart – the Philistine method. God was offended at this carnal way of accomplishing a spiritual goal. And Uzzah, the son of Abinadab, died for it.

That kind of judgment is not confined to the Old Testament. In the early days of the Church, many wealthy Christians were selling their property and donating the proceeds. A man named Joseph of Cyprus did this, and he was given the nickname, Barnabas, meaning "Son of Encouragement". A certain couple in the Church saw this and wanted a piece of that praise. Ananias and Sapphira sold a piece of property and brought the money to the apostles. But they did not give the whole amount of the sale. Was that wrong? No, the Bible makes that very clear. But they *acted* as if they had given the whole amount, in a show of false generosity. God was not going to tolerate this kind of hypocrisy in His Church.

Peter was tipped off by the Holy Spirit and confronted Ananias: "Why has Satan filled your heart to lie to the Holy Spirit?" (Acts 5:3). Ananias fell down dead on the spot. Later, his wife Sapphira came in, and Peter questioned her, too. She tried to maintain the lie. "Behold," said Peter, "the feet of those who buried your husband are at the door, and they will carry you out" (Acts 5:9). She died also, and "great fear came upon the whole church and upon all who heard of these things" (Acts 5:11). We should all be grateful that God has not done this every time someone in the Church has acted like a hypocrite over money!

God is not ultimately impressed with your acts of devotion. What He desires is actual devotion. If you try to overcome your sin with sin, you will fail. Don't try to deal in gradations of evil, pull it out by the roots.

STOP STRIVING

The solutions of Scripture do not make very much sense to most people. We cannot conceive of self-improvement with the "self" part removed. Speak of growth without effort, or victory without battle, and people don't quite know how to receive it. There are many Christians who have chosen to make the source of their sanctification their own determination. Others know that they ought not to be struggling, but are at a loss of what to do next.

If you find yourself in that place, then you have not yet come to the end of yourself. You see the monster in the mirror, but you think you can lick him. You think there is still something within yourself to be called upon to win that battle. Jacob was putting forth a lot of effort to overcome his uncle. But even as he gained wealth and status, he was stuck. Because he was striving in the flesh. He needed to stop striving and let go.

You probably hate that advice. You don't want to let go, you want to get going. But you are thinking in the flesh. You are acting as if the only things in this world were material, as if you were in complete control of your destiny. You need to open your eyes.

> "The natural man does not accept the things of the Spirit of God, for they are folly to him, and he is not able to understand them because they are spiritually discerned." (1 Corinthians 2:14)

If you desire to overcome your worst tendencies, then you need to stop thinking in the realm of your weakness. If you are the problem, then you cannot solve the problem. You need to renounce your entire perspective before you can see any improvement.

It would be easy at this point to scoff and point out the obvious fact that our problems are very real. They are "in the flesh", and demand a so-called real-world solution. But the Bible reminds us that,

> "Though we walk in the flesh, we are not waging war according to the flesh. For the weapons of our warfare are not of the flesh but have divine power to destroy strongholds." (2 Corinthians 10:3-4)

Satan totally dominates the fleshly battlefield, with strongholds everywhere. He is a master of exploiting human weaknesses. Don't fight him on his turf. There is power available to you, but it is not accessible through a worldly perspective. The body, and by extension the mind, is not your power source. It is only through reliance on God and His spiritual power that you will see deliverance.

You need to admit that what you have been doing is not working. You've tried every other way, and where has that gotten you? You're still waking up with the same issues every morning. Why not try it God's way? You've already met Him in the wilderness, He's already promised to help you. It's time to start thinking about your life His way. Stop striving. Stand still, and see the salvation of the Lord (Exodus 14:13).

The flesh is so pervasive and so convincing. We are thoroughly convinced that the only real things are made of flesh, blood, bone, earth, wind, fire, time and space. It can take a lot of unlearning to realize the truth. Jacob had to go through decades of struggle until he was burned-out enough to believe. How long is it going to take you?

STUDY QUESTIONS

1.) What is it in the heart of a revolutionary that can doom the cause of freedom? How important is it to have the right heart in doing the right thing?

2.) Have you ever known a person like Laban? How did you handle that situation? What should you have done?

3.) Was Jacob's approach to breeding Laban's flocks a good thing or a bad thing? Could it have been both? What is the role of shrewdness in the Christian life?

4.) "Having begun by the Spirit, are you now being perfected by the flesh?" (Galatians 3:3) What was this verse originally about? How can it apply to your situation?

5.) What natural bodily needs do you indulge too much? Is it harder to resist the flesh than outside temptation?

6.) What issue are you trying to address by reading this book? Have you tried to solve this problem before? Why didn't it work?

7.) Are you more tempted to try willpower, intellect, organization, hard work, or passion to overcome your problems? Why do each of these approaches fail?

8.) Does it surprise you that God still brought water from the rock when Moses struck it instead of speaking to it? What does that teach us about "success" achieved in the flesh?

9.) What are some ways that Christians tend to use "Philistine" methods to do holy things? Which of these methods are tempting for you?

10.) Can you admit that your own attempts to fix your life have not worked so far? If your power is spiritual, not carnal, where should you direct your efforts?

8

I CAN'T TAKE IT ANYMORE!

JACOB RENOUNCES LABAN

(Genesis 31)

THAT'S ALL I CAN STANDS

Have you ever fallen down a YouTube hole? If you're unfamiliar, this is when you stumble across some weird thing on YouTube, and the next thing you know, you've watched thirty videos of dogs running through sliding-glass doors. Some of my favorites over the years have been scare-cam pranks, wisdom tooth surgeries, and *Minecraft* speed-runs. But one of my all-time favorite YouTube holes is watching bullies getting beat up by their victims.

This never gets old. Someone is right up in someone else's face, talking trash and making threats. But a point comes where the victim has had enough, hauls off and smacks the bully. The tough guy curls up in a ball or runs away, while the other guy chases him down. It's intensely satisfying to see an abusive jerk get put in his place.

What is remarkable about these videos is how much people are willing to take before standing up for themselves. Most people, it seems, would rather take the verbal abuse if they can walk away without a fight. But as an outsider, it just drives you crazy! You think to yourself, "Why don't you fight back? If you don't stand up for yourself, he's just going to keep coming!" How right we are. And yet how rare to have that same attitude toward our own vices.

Haven't you ever had a friend who let people walk all over them? Maybe it was a girl with her string of boyfriends, or a kid with his football coach. There are grown men who will not tolerate disrespect from anyone at the job, but their wives talk at them like they're nothing. You know that a change in that relationship would not only be good for them, but for the other person. But something is holding them back.

It's the same thing with sin. We let our flesh walk all over us. It might sound odd to think of being intimidated by yourself, but that's what happens. The need for a drink, a hair-trigger temper, unhealthy eating habits, the tendency to obsess over bad news – all of these things can be as domineering as the worst of mothers-in-law.

But we can be fully aware that we are stuck, and yet never get free. We can explain, dissect, and articulate our struggles to anybody who asks. And yet we never take the steps to get free. You've got to ask yourself, "Why?" What is it going to take for you to finally say with Popeye, "That's all I can stands, I can't stands no more!" Sin is a bully, and you are its victim. Don't let it steal your lunch money one more time.

This is easy to say, but I wouldn't say it if I didn't know it was possible. You've been made aware of your complicity in your life's struggle, you've been taken by God to see your current trajectory, and you've admitted that you can't fix yourself. The next step is to run. Turn around and run for your life! Run from that future version of yourself.

But you will learn, as Jacob did, that your sin is not going to let you off that easy. You need to take a stand. You need a moment when you renounce that old way of living, and turn around to go a different way. We call that repentance.

THE SHOWDOWN

Jacob lived in Haran, working for Laban for twenty years (Genesis 31:38). He made himself rich by selectively breeding Laban's flocks. His brothers-in-law resented his prosperity at their father's expense, and Laban himself had become openly hostile (Genesis 31:1-2). Jacob had overstayed his welcome.

He received a dream from the Lord, who revealed that it was He who had caused the flocks to be born to Jacob's advantage (*not* magic sticks!). Bolstered by God's favor, and His exhortation to go home, Jacob called a secret family meeting. He, Rachel and Leah all agreed they'd had enough of Laban's schemes. It was time to leave.

When "Laban had gone to shear his sheep" (Genesis 31:9), Jacob gathered his family and his belongings and made a break for it. Remember, Laban kept his flocks at three-days' distance from Jacob's. And sheep-shearing was a lively festival in this culture, so Jacob knew he could get a good head start. If he could get away without a conflict, he was going to do so.

Jacob was still the Heel-Catcher. He was trying to sneak away without a direct confrontation. But abusive people will never let you just walk away. Especially because, as it says in Genesis 31:19, "Rachel stole her father's household gods." These were small idols, unique to each family. If you've seen *Gladiator*, you have seen Maximus praying to his little statuettes, a very similar idea. But these were not just objects of worship; they were a marker of authority and prosperity. A man's *teraphim* would be passed down to his children. Perhaps this was Rachel's revenge against her father. It was an insult to his honor that Laban could not allow to pass by unanswered.

"On the third day" (Genesis 31:22), Laban heard that Jacob was gone. "He took his kinsmen with him and pursued him for seven days" (Genesis 31:23). This was not a father trying to say goodbye to his daughters, this was a posse! Laban never had any intention of letting Jacob depart. Combined with the insult of the theft of his gods, he rode with murder in his heart.

He caught up with the large caravan and got in Jacob's face. "What have you done?" he demanded (Genesis 31:26). He accused Jacob of kidnapping his family and insisted that he would have sent them off with a big party if he had only asked nicely. "It is in my power to do you harm," he threatened. But luckily for Jacob, God had appeared to Laban in a dream and forbidden him from touching Jacob or his family (Genesis 31:29). The only point of contention Laban wanted resolved was to know, "Why did you steal my gods?" (Genesis 31:30). In the words of my Uncle John: Isn't it a bummer when your gods can be stolen?

Cowardly Jacob tried to reason with this unreasonable man. He admitted to his fear of Laban, even though God was clearly fighting for him. Then he announced that anyone found to be in possession of Laban's *teraphim* would be killed, not realizing that it was Rachel!

The next thing we know, Laban is rummaging through the tents of Jacob, looking for his gods. He came to Rachel's tent, but she deceived her father by hiding them in her camel's saddle. She lied down on it and claimed that "the way of women" was upon her (Genesis 31:35). Jacob was still letting his uncle walk all over him. Laban had fooled him and manipulated him and shown up threatening to kill him. He had accused him of wrongdoing and demanded the return of something Jacob had not stolen. Now the wicked trickster was snooping around his wives' tents while one of them (as far as he knew) was on her period! When would enough be enough? How long was he going to let this guy push him around?

Finally, finally, *finally* – Jacob snapped. "Jacob became angry and berated Laban" (Genesis 31:36).

> "These twenty years I have been in your house. I served you fourteen years for your two daughters, and six years for your flock, and you have changed my wages ten times. If the God of my father, the God of Abraham and the Fear of Isaac, had not been on my side, surely now you would have sent me away empty-handed. God saw my affliction and the labor of my hands and rebuked you last night." (Genesis 31:41-42)

Jacob was finally willing to stand on the favor of the Lord and renounce Laban to his face.

Did Laban learn his lesson? Of course not. "All that you see is mine," he insisted (Genesis 31:43). But he knew he was beaten. So he and Jacob made a pillar of stones as a memorial and swore that neither one would cross that marker to come against the other. This is the equivalent of telling your squabbling kids to sit on opposite sides of the car. But it was enough.

> "Early in the morning Laban arose and kissed his grandchildren and his daughters and blessed them. Then Laban departed and returned home." (Genesis 31:55)

Good riddance.

TURN AROUND AND CHANGE YOUR MIND

This was the reason for Jacob's journey into the wilderness. Yes, he was forced to leave because of his family situation. Yes, this was Rebekah's way of ensuring he did not marry a Canaanite woman. And yes, God was using this time to bless him and establish trust in His Covenant. But personally, this journey was meant to show Jacob where his deception could lead, and to push him to the point of saying, "Enough".

When we sin, we feel bad. We know we have done something wrong, so our conscience stings. But it's easy to just sleep it off and move on. We try to work on the problem, rather than fixing the cause of the problem. That is why God brought Jacob to Laban. Jacob was a Heel-Catcher. Maybe he wasn't proud of it, but he might not have seen the dangerous possibilities of that identity. Maybe he saw it as the only way to navigate a hostile world. Maybe he thought it was fun to be tricky. Or maybe he truly didn't know anything else.

So God allowed him to get kicked around by an even greater Heel-Catcher for twenty years. Jacob felt the pain of dealing with a sneaky, deceptive person like himself. Finally, he wanted out. He wanted to get away from Laban. And in a symbolic sense, he wanted to get away from living that life. Lying, sneaking and cheating had brought him nothing but trouble. It was time to leave.

The Bible calls us to renounce our sin and flesh and to begin anew in obedience to God. The word for this is "repentance". It's one of those Christian words to which we grow accustomed, but we need to make sure we understand it.

I'll never forget, the first person to get saved under my ministry was a girl named Sara. I taught on the crucifixion and issued numerous calls to "repent". She came up after the service and very simply asked me what repentance was. I explained that to repent meant to renounce your old life and commit to a new one under God's direction. Once she understood that, she was ready. She repented and believed on the Lord Jesus Christ that very day.

You too must repent. It's not just a street sign held up by obnoxious Christians. It was in fact the defining message of Jesus' ministry.

"From that time Jesus began to preach, saying, 'Repent, for the kingdom of heaven is at hand.'" (Matthew 4:17)

It is also the message of the Church, given by Christ Himself:

"Thus it is written, that the Christ should suffer and on the third day rise from the dead, and that repentance for the forgiveness of sins should be proclaimed in his name to all nations." (Luke 24:47)

There are two words from two languages in the Bible that both translate "repent" or "repentance". These two definitions together give us a full picture of what we're talking about. Of what you must do to the bully of your sin and flesh.

The Old Testament was written in Hebrew, with a few short parts in Aramaic. The Hebrew word for repent is *shuv*. This is a very simple word that just means to "turn" or to "turn away". It can mean to "return," depending on the context. Taken spiritually, this means to turn away from wickedness, and turn to the Lord. And if you have backslidden, it means to "return" unto God, like the prodigal son. Ezekiel prophesied,

> "Repent and turn away from your idols, and turn away your faces from all your abominations." (Ezekiel 14:6)

You can see the picture here, to stop looking to dumb idols for salvation and instead to turn to the Lord.

This is what Jacob did in leaving Haran. He quite literally turned away from Laban and began to return home. Symbolically, he turned away from his life as a Heel-Catcher and turned to the Lord, who had a better future planned for him. This is what must be done when we realize the terrible person we could become. Turn and walk the other way. If you knew that you were heading for the edge of a cliff with your foot on the gas, you would stop and turn around immediately. The same must be done morally and spiritually. Where is your life going? Is that somewhere you want to end up? Time to turn around.

The New Testament was written in Greek, and the word it uses for repentance is *metanoia*. This word means a change of mind, to think differently, to leave old thoughts behind. If you change your direction, but follow the same GPS settings, you are going to end up at the same old place. So Paul urged the Romans to,

"Be transformed by the renewal of your mind, that by testing you may discern what is the will of God, what is good and acceptable and perfect." (Romans 12:2)

Our old patterns of thought are no good for us. They are corrupted by sin, and they have not born good fruit. You must agree with God that your way isn't working and choose to think about your life His way. That is the second component of repentance.

This is what Jacob failed to do when he ran away from Laban. He wanted to get away from him, but he did not change his approach. The whole process was one of passivity and deception. The secret meeting in the field, waiting for the sheep-shearing to begin, not saying a word to anyone, and allowing Laban to talk down to him and even search his tents. It was not until Jacob was willing to confront Laban to his face and insist upon his rights and upon God's favor that he was able to be rid of Laban. He needed to think differently, not just walk away.

True repentance is a combination of right belief and right action. The renunciation of oneself involves not just a change of direction, but a change of mind. Try to do one without the other, and you'll find yourself stalling out. *Shuv* and *metanoia* – repentance.

SIN SNOWBALLS

I usually get my hair cut at a place called Sport Clips. You can pay extra for something called the MVP treatment. After cutting your hair, they'll offer you a shampoo, a hot towel, and a quick shoulder massage. Always relaxing! But a certain friend of mine, who shall remain nameless, had a rather different experience at Sport Clips.

He came to me one day, ready to rant about this really weird barbershop he went to. He said that after they cut his hair, the lady led him into a back room where the lights were low, and told him to lay down. "She started *washing* my hair!" he said, disbelievingly. "Then she put this burning hot towel on my face, and used this massager thing on my shoulders!" When you first come to Sport Clips, they offer you the MVP for free. Apparently, this woman did not tell my friend what was going to happen, and just walked him through the process. He couldn't figure out what had happened to him! But I knew right away, and I could not stop laughing. "How far were you willing to let them go before questioning it?" I laughed.

That's a funny story, but it helps illustrate the point of this chapter. How far are you going to let your sin take you before you stop and ask a few questions? We read the story of Jacob and Laban and we can't believe that he would put up with this man for so long. But what about you? Have you allowed your sinful habits to back you into a corner, to take you to a place you never thought you'd end up?

Alcoholics never take that first drink hoping that they will turn into a spousal abuser, or crash into a minivan while under the influence. Businessmen who fudge the numbers for the first time never plan on embezzling millions of dollars and bankrupting their company. Men who lust after other women never expect to end up frequenting strip clubs or breaking their wife's heart. And teenagers who sleep around rarely consider the possibilities of children coming along. But wisdom dictates that we consider these things long before we get there.

At what stage of the process are you now? Maybe you've hit your crisis moment, but do you realize that it could still get much, much worse? Or does God need to provide you with a few more examples? Sin snowballs. Your little vices are not cute, they're not part of what makes you beautiful, and they're not manageable. They are bullies, pushing you to do things you would never do with a clear head. It's time to repent.

First, you've got to change your mind, *metanoia*. You've got to completely alter the way you think about yourself. The terrible things that you have inflicted on other people, however unintentionally, are not rare exceptions. They are the fruit that comes from the seeds you've planted. Maybe you've never even put much thought into your beliefs and behavior. It's time to start. It's time to let God's standards replace yours, because His are timeless and perfect, while yours are erroneous and dangerous.

This means examining your motivations and your attributes. If you were given a descriptive name, would it be something like "Heel-Catcher"? Maybe you think of yourself as the party animal, and that identity has trapped you. Change your mind, change your self-perception. Maybe you think of yourself as the strong, self-reliant one, and you've driven away everyone who's ever loved you. That's not how God sees you, stop thinking of yourself that way. Are you the one who's smarter than everyone else, and your arrogance has gotten you into trouble again? *Metanoia*.

Second, you've got to change your direction, *shuv*. You can't keep living the way you're living. You might agree that your direction is a bad one, but if you don't do anything about it, things will only get worse. There can be fear attached to a move like this, Jacob was afraid. Some people are so addicted to playing the victim because of their miserable past, they don't even want to move on. But God will give you courage if you ask Him. You don't need another emotional breakthrough, you need to put feet to your intentions and *shuv*.

This is different for every situation, but it isn't complicated. Stop doing the wrong thing! Are you cheating on your spouse? Break it off immediately. Are you passive-aggressive and manipulative to your family? Start speaking plainly and stop brooding. Are you full of rage and pride in your online interactions? Quit social media. You'll survive, I promise. Have you tried to make your way through life without God? Bow the knee and repent. It is the only way to be saved.

There are those who try to downplay the moment of decision. And there is some wisdom in that. John the Baptist refused to baptize some of the religious leaders when they came. He told them first to, "bear fruits in keeping with repentance" (Luke 3:8), because he knew how hypocritical they were. But I think it is important to have a "face-to-face with Laban" moment, if you know what I mean. You can't just be looking for God to get you out of a jam, or help you manage your mistakes. You've got to have a point in your life when you turn around, change your mind, and start going the other way.

If you can never reach the point where enough is enough, then sin will keep pushing you around, while everyone around you wonders why you don't do something about it. Meanwhile, things will get worse. You'll do things that would shock a younger you. But these won't be surprising to God. They will be another step in an inevitable journey – one that you could stop at any moment.

NEVER TOO LATE

My favorite example of repentance in the Bible is that of Manasseh. He was the son of Hezekiah, one of the best kings Judah ever had. But Manasseh was not like his father.

> "He did what was evil in the sight of the Lord, according to the despicable practices of the nations whom the Lord drove out before the people of Israel." (2 Kings 21:2)

He rebuilt the pagan altars his father had torn down, worshiping the stars of heaven, even building false altars in the Temple itself. He was a magician, dealing with necromancers and witches. Worst of all, he sacrificed his own son as an offering, probably to the Canaanite god Molech. With good reason then did God announce that because of Manasseh, "I will wipe Jerusalem as one wipes a dish, wiping it and turning it upside down" (2 Kings 21:13).

God brought the Assyrians against the land of Judah, "who captured Manasseh with hooks and bound him with chains of bronze and brought him to Babylon" (2 Chronicles 33:11). That reference to "hooks" describes the Assyrian practice of putting sharp hooks into the skin of their captives (through the nose especially) and dragging them forward in a humiliating procession. You might say Manasseh got what he deserved.

"[But] when he was in distress, he entreated the favor of the Lord his God and humbled himself greatly before the God of his fathers. He prayed to him, and God was moved by his entreaty and heard his plea, and brought him again to Jerusalem into his kingdom. Then Manasseh knew that the Lord was God." (2 Chronicles 33:12-13)

God forgave Manasseh when he repented! He was restored to his throne, and when he returned, he undid all that he had done before. He removed the idols and strengthened the city in the name of the Lord. What a turnaround! The witch-king of Israel, the arrogant idolater, was forgiven and restored when he repented.

God is so willing to forgive those who renounce their old lives, that sometimes it makes the rest of us angry. You remember the story of Zacchaeus, that "wee little man" who wanted to see Jesus. Zacchaeus was a tax collector. He collaborated with Rome, the oppressors of Israel, to take his people's money and enrich himself. He was the equivalent of a Nazi collaborator in Poland during World War II. But he had heard of Jesus, and wanted to see Him. So he climbed up in a sycamore tree to watch Him as He came into Jericho.

> "And when Jesus came to the place, he looked up and said to him, 'Zacchaeus, hurry and come down, for I must stay at your house today.'" (Luke 19:5)

Jesus is asking to share a meal with a tax collector. When the rest of the crowd saw this, "they all grumbled, 'He has gone in to be the guest of a man who is a sinner'" (Luke 19:7). They wanted Jesus to be their political liberator, but He was only interested in saving souls. At the dinner, Zacchaeus swore to repay everything he had stolen five times, and to give half of everything he owned to the poor. Talk about a change of direction! As Jesus said that day, "the Son of Man came to seek and to save the lost" (Luke 19:10).

One other story from the life of Jesus came when He was eating dinner at a Pharisee's house. During the meal, a woman, "who was a sinner" (Luke 7:37), came to Jesus and anointed His feet with an expensive perfume. She began to weep, reduced to wiping the tears from his feet with her hair. This woman was so overwhelmed by Jesus' message of forgiveness and love that she couldn't contain herself.

> "[But] when the Pharisee who had invited him saw this, he said to himself, 'If this man were a prophet, he would have known who and what sort of woman this is who is touching him, for she is a sinner.'" (Luke 7:39)

When we decide to make a change, other people will doubt and deride us, knowing only what we have been before. But Jesus sees what we could be. That is the reason He allows us to see where we are going. He wants us to repent and follow His better way. That's His kindness at work (Romans 2:4). Jesus said that a person who has been forgiven much will love much, while those who only feel they have been forgiven a little, will only show a little love (Luke 7:47). The moment you are ready to repent, Jesus will be there to receive you and to guide you into the life He has planned for you.

THIS IS NOT OPTIONAL

Repentance is the renunciation of your old self, and the embrace of your new life in Christ. So far, I have been speaking mostly in terms of the benefit to you. But I ought to make it abundantly clear that this is not just a matter of a better life. Repentance is non-negotiable.

> "If a man does not repent, God will whet his sword; he has bent and readied his bow; he has prepared for him his deadly weapons, making his arrows fiery shafts." (Psalm 7:12-13)

Why is God so violently opposed to a lack of repentance? Because, as it says in the verse prior,

> "God is a righteous judge, and a God who feels indignation every day." (Psalm 7:11)

We've been talking about Jacob, and how he wrecked his own life. But what about his family's life? What about Isaac, who was taken advantage of by his own child? What about Rebekah, whose marriage was left in shambles? What about Esau? What about the Promise? Jacob had jeopardized all of that, and was still doing the same kinds of things in Haran. How could God allow that kind of man to wander the earth without doing something about it?

How can God allow a man or woman like you to wander the earth, with all the pain you have brought into it? God is kind. He knows the pain that your sin brings you. He would rather see your life turned around and your mind changed so that you might be an agent of change, a spreader of love and joy. But you first must renounce that old way of living that leads only to destruction. That's what the Gospel is all about:

> "The grace of God has appeared, bringing salvation for all people, training us to renounce ungodliness and worldly passions, and to live self-controlled, upright, and godly lives in the present age."
> (Titus 2:12-13)

We have such a bad habit of identifying ourselves with our temptations and sins. That is of the Devil, not God speaking to you. Even if you have been saved for a long time, it's time to stop letting sin run your life. Stop letting Laban rummage through your luggage, he has no business there! Whether it's a major malfunction, or just the beginnings of a bad habit, you must repent. Change the way you are thinking, and change the direction in which you are walking. Leave Haran and go home. Renounce yourself and move on.

STUDY QUESTIONS

1.) How does it feel to watch someone get pushed around? When you see it, what do you wish they would do?

2.) Do you have any besetting sins or bad habits that you have struggled with for a long time? Why do we allow such things to continue for so long?

3.) Why did Jacob let Laban talk to him so roughly, even after God had told Laban not to touch him? What does this say about Jacob's character?

4.) What are examples of influences that we should not allow in our lives? Why do we let them do so anyway?

5.) Why does God allow us to be exhausted by our sin? Is it possible to speed up this process?

6.) There are two words for repentance, meaning to change your mind and change your direction. What is the danger of only changing your mind? What about only changing your direction?

7.) Are you currently letting a person, or a situation, or a memory push you around? How far has it gone? Is it hard to admit this? Why not put a stop to it right now?

8.) Jacob was trapped by his identity as the "Heel-Catcher". What identity or label has you trapped? What would happen if you dropped that label?

9.) Are you encouraged by the repentance of Manasseh? Is it ever too late to repent? If God would forgive him, or Zacchaeus, why not you?

10.) Read Psalm 7:11-13 again. Do you agree that your current trajectory will be damaging to your family, your country, the world and yourself? If that is true, what steps would be too drastic to put a stop to it?

9

YOU'VE GOT TO GO BACK

JACOB RETURNS HOME

(Genesis 32:1-12)

NON NOBIS TANTUM NATI

On a whim, I once decided to trace my family history. I'd always been a little skeptical about this since everybody's family tree seems to end up at Queen Victoria or William the Conqueror. But I wanted to follow the fatherly line without deviation. Due to the abundance of information on the Internet now, I was able to connect our living memory with a tremendous account written by someone else, taking us all the way back to the old country, with tantalizing hints about what came before.

My family came to America in 1633 as part of a Puritan group that would found Hartford, Connecticut (then Massachusetts). Later, they moved to Pennsylvania to be part of the Moravian community there. Two of my ancestors refused to fight in the American Revolution and were sentenced to hard labor. The family went west to Ohio with other Moravians until the Civil War. An ancestor fought for the Union, and the family was adrift for generations after that, eventually settling in California, where my grandfather was able to pick up the story.

But before any of that, the Warners were landowners in Essex, England. We had a coat of arms, a crest, and everything. And I discovered our ancient family creed, forgotten until this very decade: *Non nobis tantum nati*. That's Latin. It means, "We are not born for ourselves alone". My family had forgotten those words over the generations, but it's my intention to remember them.

Is that not an idea to aspire to? To live not just for yourself, but to see yourself as born with great responsibility. If everyone in your family would take on that attitude, what changes might there be? If everyone in the nation would see themselves as part of a whole, is there any limit to what we might accomplish? *Non nobis tantum nati*. This is the next step in our journey: the return.

We have followed Jacob as he was thrust out into the wilderness because of his failure. The wilderness, you remember, is a picture of training and transformation. Along the way, we met God, and He took us into the depths of ourselves to face the monster in the mirror. By now, hopefully you have repented of that attitude, and determined to submit to God's leadership away from that terrible future.

As much as we'd like it to be, this is not the end of the story. Many other programs of self-actualization are satisfied to make you a better person. But God is wiser. He knows that having a moment of personal catharsis, or choosing to do better from now on is not enough. You've got to go back. You must return to the mess that you made, the people that messed you up, and repair what has been broken. This is perhaps the scariest part of the journey.

It would be easy to learn your lesson and try to forget what came before. But *non nobis tantum nati.* You were born for more than yourself. You owe it to those whom you have hurt – and those who have hurt you – to return as a new man and try to make it right. This calls for humility, and it calls for courage.

FEAR AS A COMPASS

With Laban in the rearview mirror, Jacob and his family moved on to Canaan. As they reached the ford where they would cross the Jordan River, "the angels of God met him" (Genesis 32:1). It's not clear if this was a vision or a dream, but Jacob observed the armies of God encamped at his destination. "And when Jacob saw them he said, 'This is God's camp!' So he called the name of that place Mahanaim" (Genesis 32:2), which means "Two Camps" in Hebrew. It was God who had told Jacob it was time to go home, and He had promised to be with him. It must have been a boost to Jacob's spirits to see a troop of angels waiting at the entrance to the Promised Land. He now knew for sure that God had led him to this place.

It was assurance that came not a moment too soon. Up to this point, the only thought occupying Jacob's mind was to get away from Laban. He was afraid, and with good reason. His uncle had intended to kill him, after all. But now that the crisis with Laban was past, Jacob could turn his eyes to the future. And that prospect was even more intimidating than the one he had just escaped.

Remember, he had defrauded his brother of his birthright by deceiving his father at the behest of his mother. The last words he had heard from Esau were a vow to kill him the moment Isaac died, to take

173

the blessing from him anyway. The trust between him and his parents was gone, but the more pressing issue was certainly the looming death threat from Esau. And so, bolstered by the attending angels at Mahanaim, "Jacob sent messengers before him to Esau his brother in the land of Seir, the country of Edom" (Genesis 32:3), explaining that he had returned from Laban a wealthy man. "I have sent to tell my lord," he said, "in order that I may find favor in your sight" (Genesis 32:5).

Esau had left Canaan to seek his fortune in the deserts to the south. He had conquered the rocky terrain of what came to be called "Edom" in his honor. Jacob's violent brother was a warlord now, so he wisely sent emissaries to announce his arrival. This was good! He was behaving forthrightly and acting like a man. His repentance appears to have been genuine. But his fortitude was about to be tested.

> "The messengers returned to Jacob, saying, 'We came to your brother Esau, and he is coming to meet you, and there are four hundred men with him." (Genesis 32:6)

This was no welcome party. This was a war party. Esau was coming to settle the score – at least, that's how Jacob took it. As you can imagine, "Jacob was greatly afraid and distressed" (Genesis 32:7). His worst nightmare was coming true. All the self-convincing he had done, hoping that Esau's temper would have cooled seemed so foolish now.

He began to divide his belongings and people into two camps, so that at least they wouldn't all die. And then he did a very sensible thing. He began to pray. He began by addressing the Lord as the one who had told him to return home. He thanked God for all His blessings, and then got to the point:

174

"Please deliver me from the hand of my brother, from the hand of Esau, for I fear him, that he may come and attack me, the mothers with the children." (Genesis 32:11)

Lifelong fear threatened to unman the man of God. But he ended his prayer by putting his situation into God's hands.

"But you said, 'I will surely do you good, and make your offspring as the sand of the sea, which cannot be numbered for multitude.'" (Genesis 32:12)

In essence, he said: "God, you got me into this mess. You told me to come home. You promised that you would bless me with innumerable descendants. Esau wants to kill me. So it's up to you to save me!" This might not have been the bravest of prayers, but at least he was praying. The moment of truth had come, and Jacob was facing it head-on (so far!). He would need a little more convincing in the next verses, but for now it is enough for us to see that he was making a legitimate effort to change. He had submitted to God, finally, and God led him right to where he did not want to go. Jacob was terrified. But that's the thing about fear. Sometimes it can be a pretty great compass for exactly where we need to go.

THE COST OF DISCIPLESHIP

When we have an encounter with God, it can be incredibly cathartic. Letting go of an emotional burden, committing afresh to righteous living, or even the initial moment of salvation. These moments are like being set free from slavery and death. But when the celebration dies down, we can usually feel the tug of the Holy Spirit

175

guiding us to a place we do not want to go. In many cases, that is "back home". We may have been personally changed, but that change places a responsibility upon us to set things right.

Very often, the most painful parts of our lives are the last ones to be sanctified. God works to renew our language, our thought life, even our bank account. But there sits a broken relationship with a parent, or a vain addiction to social media, or a church that you left in shambles. These are the matters that God wants to set right. You have a duty to shine a light into the darkest corners of your heart to uncover what is there and set it to rights.

Do not think that God will give you a pass on this. When people came to see Jesus, He welcomed them with open arms if they were repentant. But He also had a keen eye for halfway-ism, and He would not allow people to duck their duty. The cost of discipleship is everything that you have. As Jesus Himself said,

> "If anyone would come after me, let him deny himself and take up his cross and follow me. For whoever would save his life will lose it, but whoever loses his life for my sake will find it." (Matthew 16:24-25)

Most of us are willing to give most of us, but Jesus requires all of us. Consider this string of stories from the Gospel of Luke 9:57-62.

One man said to Jesus, "I will follow you wherever you go."

Wow, isn't that great? Not exactly.

Jesus responded, "Foxes have holes, and birds of the air have nests, but the Son of Man has nowhere to lay his head."

What's that all about? Jesus knew this man was unwilling to leave his comfort and stability behind, and so that became, for him, the cost of discipleship. Jesus was right. The man was never heard from again.

To the second man, Jesus extended an invitation: "Follow me." What a privilege to have the Lord Himself ask you to be His disciple!

But the man said, "Lord, let me first go and bury my father."

This was not just permission to attend the funeral. This man was asking for a delay until after his father died, probably to avoid the inevitable confrontation. What did Jesus have to say?

"Leave the dead to bury their own dead. But as for you, go and proclaim the kingdom of God."

His excuse was not good enough for Jesus. The displeasure of that man's father was the cost of his discipleship, but he was not willing to pay.

A third said, "I will follow you, Lord, but let me first say farewell to those at my home."

Now, this seems eminently reasonable. Why not let this guy bid his family adieu?

But Jesus replied, "No one who puts his hand to the plow and looks back is fit for the kingdom of God."

This man was looking to maintain a connection with the old life, just in case this whole Messiah thing didn't work out. Jesus wouldn't let him get away with it. The cost of discipleship was a complete severance from his old life, nothing else would be acceptable.

Why did Jesus place obstacles in the way of prospective disciples? Because salvation is not about fixing your own issues at your own pace. It is death to self, renunciation of the old life. Whatever your line in the sand, that is the line you must cross to be saved. And that means shouldering the burden of the mess that drove you into the wilderness in the first place. The one thing Jacob did not want to do was to return home and confront Esau. But that was the one thing that needed to be done to heal his soul and complete his transformation. The confrontation with Esau was, in a manner of speaking, the price of admission into the life God had promised him at Bethel.

So many have gone through the motions of repentance and obedience, only to break away at the last second, unwilling to take the final step. There's a man like that in the Gospel of Mark. He is known to us as the rich young ruler.

He ran up to Jesus and asked, "Good Teacher, what must I do to inherit eternal life?" (Mark 10:17).

That's a good question to ask. Maybe it's the same question that caused you to pick up this book. Jesus ran the young man through the Ten Commandments, and he claimed that he had kept them all. Perhaps this was true. But we all have a breaking point. And that was where Jesus took him next.

> "Jesus, looking at him, loved him" – that is always the heart that God has for broken people – "and said to him, 'You lack one thing: go, sell all that you have and give to the poor, and you will have treasure in heaven; and come, follow me.'" (Mark 10:21)

Is everyone required to sell all they have to follow Jesus? No. But this man was. Because it was the one thing that he was unwilling to do. It represented the greed and avarice and insecurity that was rotting out the base of his heart. Jesus put his finger right on the sore spot, and made that the cost of his discipleship. Once again, Jesus was shown to be wise. For, "disheartened by the saying, he went away sorrowful, for he had great possessions" (Mark 10:22).

The rich young ruler knew he had a problem. He was willing to take a journey into the wilderness, even to meet with God. He was prepared to believe whatever he needed to, no doubt even to denounce the love of money. But he could not return home and make a change. His epiphany would not last the drive home from church that day. And that is why Jesus would not welcome him as a disciple.

What does it cost to realize the life God has planned for you? Everything. It's different for every person. For one, it is the selling of his possessions, for another it is a fearful confrontation with his murderous brother. But whatever it is, it must be done, or the journey into the wilderness will have been in vain.

WHO'S GOING TO CLEAN UP THIS MESS?

The hero always has to come home. This is part of any good story. Simba cannot lounge about in paradise, he must return to the Pride Lands. Jake in *Avatar* cannot just abandon the Na'vi, he must help them in their desperate battle. The Pevensie children have to return from Narnia. No story is complete without the final battle, and the same is true for you.

Whether you entered the wilderness on the heels of a terrible crisis, or undertook the journey in order to prevent one, once you have met God and renounced the old life, it is time to go back. And while it might seem valorous to stage a last stand in some epic movie, our own struggles are far more mundane. We deal in the realm of rebellious children and compulsive habits. Yet the confrontation is no less important for its small scale.

If the mess has already been made, it is easier to begin. If you were already caught lying, it's pretty clear where you need to begin. Maybe there are people who have been hurt, or trust that has been broken, dreams that have been shattered. You must go about repairing each one of these things. It's not enough to "learn your lesson" and move on. Fail to address the problem head-on, and you'll regret it forever.

As a rule, the scarier the step you must take, the more important it is to your spiritual wellbeing. You must take courage in the fact that it is God who brought you here. Think back on the calling He has given you. Remember that your life matters, and that your impact can be greater than you've ever dreamed. Look around and see the angels of the Lord camped at the entrance to your Promised Land. This is right where you need to be.

These can be small steps, to be sure. Perhaps you spend frivolously and cannot get ahead because of your impulsivity. Now you have over-drafted your bank account once again. Your "return home" would involve sitting down and making a budget. It also might involve apologizing to some people, and setting new boundaries with friends who will mock you for your diligence.

Or they can be big steps. Your marriage is falling apart because you have been a workaholic. Your wife feels like your housekeeper and babysitter, and your kids are starting to resent you. Maybe you've mouthed off and shouted them down when they've tried to talk to you about it. But do you really want to sacrifice your family on the altar of ambition? This will start with apologies, and a willingness to endure the tongue-lashing. You'll need to keep that humility over weeks and months as everyone around you taunts your attempts to turn over a new leaf. It could involve a reduction in hours at work, which might include a reduction in pay, or a loss of status at your place of employment. It's not until it starts to sting that you will see real results.

Sometimes the necessary corrections will precipitate a crisis rather than prevent one. Unstable structures do not like pressure, which is why they need to come down and be rebuilt. This is a frightful process, and the person who starts it will usually take a lot of heat.

Family dynamics can be this way. Mom rules the roost by guilting everyone with her complaints and needling comments. Dad clams up and says nothing. Everyone goes along with it, but complains behind her back and engages in small, petty acts of revenge. This has got to stop. Trouble is, everyone is used to it. Breaking the status quo would just upset her more. But it must be done. Someone's got to stand up and refuse to be bullied. There will be fights, Dad will get angry, unforgivable things will be said. It will feel worse than before. But the one who has the courage to try and bring a little sanity to that Thanksgiving table may just be the one to forge a new attitude of love and understanding out of all that dysfunction.

The examples go on and on. When are you going to stand up to your manager and tell her that you cannot keep pulling these overtime shifts? When are you as a pastor going to stop preaching hostile messages to keep the bloodthirsty crowds happy? When are you as a wife going to start providing your husband an escape from sexual temptation? When are you as a citizen going to stand up against creeping prejudice in your community? When are you going to finally lay down your childhood daydreams and start living the real life right in front of you?

God will be with you, but you must do this alone. Don't expect the people involved to celebrate your courage, at least not right away. Jesus went home to Nazareth to preach in the synagogue, and they despised Him for His supposed pretension.

"A prophet is not without honor except in his hometown and in his own household," Jesus said. (Matthew 13:57)

There was a young man in my youth group who came home from a summer retreat and apologized to his parents for his bad attitude. He promised to do better, but his dad only scoffed, "I give it a week". Can you endure past that? Can you do the right thing without any applause, like Atticus Finch in *To Kill a Mockingbird*? You must.

You might be the only person who can repair what has been broken. Even if you were not the cause of the mess you were born into, you can be the one to clean it up. Rebekah was as guilty as Jacob in his deception, but it was Jacob who needed to confront Esau. There are people who will listen only to you, there are solutions that only you can come up with. God has given gifts of His Spirit specifically to you, so that you could return from the wilderness and do the hard thing.

STUMBLING AND STUTTERING

If all this intimidates you, take heart. Many heroes of the faith have been afraid to go home. I know we keep coming back to Moses, but he really is the best example. After a great failure followed by forty years in exile, God appeared to him in the burning bush. He commanded Moses to return to Egypt and lead his people out of slavery. Five times, Moses objected. First he questioned his fitness, but God swore to be with him. Second he asked God's name, and God revealed it to him. Third, he asked for a sign, and God gave him three. Fourth, he claimed to be a poor speaker, but God reminded him who made his tongue. Finally, Moses simply said, "Oh my Lord, please send someone else" (Exodus 4:13).

That was the sticking point. Moses may have been concerned about those other things, but God saw them as mere excuses. It boiled down to the fact that Moses was afraid and did not want to go. He would have to face a warrant for his arrest, and a suspicious Hebrew nation. He was a shepherd now, an abomination to the Egyptians, and had lost whatever leadership skills he might have once had. But this was the reason he was alive. The humility and faith he had learned in the wilderness were not just for him alone. God was going to use this newly-forged Moses to lead His people on the same journey.

Sometimes we want to have our encounter with God, and then keep the encounter going forever. But that is no way to change the world. There was a man in the land of the Gerasenes who was filled with demons. He lived naked in the tombs, he cut himself and howled in the night. He could not be bound with ropes or chains, and was known only as "Legion" for the number of demons within him. But Jesus drove the evil spirits out of him with a word, and he was immediately in his right mind. Problem was, Jesus had sent the demons into a herd of pigs, which had promptly run off a cliff into the lake. So the local populace (which seemed to care more about their herds than this man) asked Jesus to leave right away.

"The man from whom the demons had gone begged that he might be with him." (Luke 8:38)

I can imagine so! Why wouldn't he want to stay with Jesus and leave all of these small-minded people behind?

"But Jesus sent him away, saying, 'Return to your home, and declare how much God has done for you.'" (Luke 8:38-39)

Jesus had a better idea. He wanted this man to testify to those who had known him as a demoniac about the wondrous forgiveness of Christ. The man did just that, and the next time Jesus returned to that

183

region, the people were excited and ready to receive Him. This man's testimony was needed in his hometown. Who else could have wrought such a change?

Sometimes home comes back to you. Joseph had been a slave and a prisoner, but was elevated to the right hand of Pharaoh. He ruled over Egypt with a kind and wise hand. At last, all of the pain of his childhood was over. He named his first child Manasseh, which meant "Forgotten", because he had finally moved on.

Or so he thought. One day, in came his ten brothers seeking to buy grain from him. Joseph freaked out. He accused them of spying and threw them in prison. Then he sent them back with their money, and feasted with them when they returned. He wept, he stuttered, and had them all arrested again! Joseph thought he had his whole life under control, but there was one corner of his heart that had not been dealt with yet. That was the corner God wanted to heal. So He brought the confrontation to Joseph's front door. Through forgiveness and love, Joseph was able to bring harmony back to the family of Israel.

You too may stutter and stumble your way through this process. But you've got to trust that there are "Two Camps" here. One is your own, your skills and experiences and talents. The other is God's and His infinite resources. With that perspective in mind, you can trust that your small little voice can be enough to command mountains to step aside (Matthew 21:21).

STRENGTHEN YOUR BROTHERS

On the night of the Last Supper, Jesus prophesied that Peter would deny Him three times. Satan was going to sift him like wheat to see if there was anything of substance behind his bluster and bravado. But Jesus had faith in Peter. "I have prayed for you," He said. And He gave

Peter instructions for what to do after he had gone through the terrible crucible of that night:

> "When you have turned again, strengthen your brothers." (Luke 22:32)

Jesus knew that Peter would fail. But He saw to the other side of that failure. He knew that Peter would learn his lesson and be a better man for it. And so before the test even began, Jesus was telling Peter what he needed to do when the night was over: "Strengthen your brothers". That same call resounds to each of us.

Non nobis tantum nati – "We are not born for ourselves alone". I might add, we are not *born again* for ourselves alone. The lessons you learn in the wilderness are not just nice memories for you to ponder. They are to be given legs, put into action to strengthen your brothers. The world needs a person like you, changed in the ways that only God can change you, working to bring about the same changes in others.

What if Elijah had gone to the brook Cherith but never returned to challenge Ahab at Mount Carmel? What if Paul had received his profound insights into the Gospel in Arabia, but never consented to preach at Antioch? What if the early Church had been filled with the Spirit on the Day of Pentecost, yet never left the four walls of the Upper Room? Tragic, selfish, pointless – I can think of a few other words we might use in such situations.

Don't make that mistake. God doesn't just want to rescue you from your terrible situation, He wants to forge you into the person who will remedy that terrible situation. He doesn't just want to make you moral, He wants to make you an agent of change in the world around you. Repentance entails a commitment to take up the burden for your life.

It might be tempting like the disciples on the Mount of Transfiguration to pitch a tent and stay up there (Matthew 17:4), but that's not what is needed. You've got to go back.

Of course, it sounds all well and good to say that when the emotions are running hot, and you're pumped up from a fresh motivational sermon. But then you have to dial that phone number, and the fear finds you. Worse still, you take the initiative, and Esau rides out to meet you with an army. In those moments, you must remember that God is with you. He allowed Jacob to see the angelic camp so that he would know that God had indeed brought him to this place. Even so, God has brought you here, to the very threshold of your Promised Land. Will you flee back into the wilderness? Or are you going to saddle up and go slay some giants?

STUDY QUESTIONS

1.) Consider the phrase, "We are not born for ourselves alone". Do you think this is true? Has your life been reflecting that belief?

2.) Very often our Christian lives are described as personal endeavors. How important is it to take other people into consideration? Does this make the process easier or more difficult for you?

3.) How must Jacob have felt when he learned Esau was riding after him with an army? Do you think he felt God had tricked him? Have you ever felt that way?

4.) What parts of your life have been easy to hand over to God? What parts have been difficult?

5.) Does it surprise you that Jesus turned people away who asked to follow Him? What does this tell us about what it means to be a disciple? What would Jesus have asked you to give up? Would you have done it?

6.) What examples can you think of from literature, movies or pop culture in which the hero had to return home? Why is this theme so common?

7.) What do you think of the idea of fear as a compass? Do you avoid the most difficult steps of spiritual growth? What scares you now?

8.) Have you ever made a spiritual commitment only to have people laugh at you or get angry? What did you do? Could you endure that again?

9.) How must Joseph have felt when his brothers showed up on his doorstep? Are there any areas of your past that you hope stay far away? Might God want you to return and make it right?

10.) Why must Christians take the initiative to repair broken relationships and circumstances? How is the example of Jesus instructive here? Are you following His example?

10

DEATH BEFORE LIFE

JACOB WRESTLES WITH GOD

(Genesis 32:13-29)

TIME TO DIE

It's been quite a journey through the wilderness so far. Hopefully you have learned a lot about yourself and are ready to return to the Promised Land. But if you are sharp and observant, you have seen the flaw in this process. Maybe you need to be a little cynical to see it. If you have not realized it already, it's time for some tough love.

Admitting your shortcomings and announcing an intention to change are not the same thing as actually changing. Your self-perception may be different, but you are still the same person. Jacob may have learned a thing or two about his sneaky, cowardly heart, but he was still a sneaky coward. How can we expect things to turn out differently if the only thing that has changed is our opinion of ourselves? That is why the next step is the most important and yet the most harrowing.

The return to the Promised Land requires passage through the waters. This is a symbol of death and Hell in the Bible. The curse of sin will continue to manifest itself through you by hurting others, wrecking good situations and cultivating awful addictions. The best thing for the world is for your heart to no longer exist; it needs to die. All along, God has been leading us to the point of death.

But surely God did not bring us out of Egypt just to kill us in the wilderness! We are not fatalists who believe that the best thing for the world is the demise of humanity. We want to see things turned around, starting with us. So we must die – and yet we must live. But is that even possible? Is there a way for us to die to the old life and be reborn to a new one?

There is. You must allow God to baptize you, to bring you under and out of the waters. Only He can put to death and raise to life in a single breath. He is the one who "gives life to the dead and calls into existence the things that do not exist" (Romans 4:17). And through His Son, He has made provision for that exact transformation.

If you have tried to avoid the "religious" aspects of this journey so far, then you have gone as far as you can go. You have reached the limits of human ability, your efforts will be inadequate beyond this point. Only God can help you now.

But I must warn you! Passing through the waters is not a light thing. You cannot cross with your family, you cannot carry any possessions. Anything that remains of your old life, your hopes, your passions, even your name must be washed away in that flood. You've got to lose everything to enter the Promised Land. Many a man has gone right up to the borders of Zion and yet refused to cross the river.

You are in great danger, even as you stand on the brink of your greatest opportunity. Choose to save your life, and you will lose it (Mark 8:35). You will be doomed to wander in the wilderness, unable to return, too afraid to move forward.

But you've come too far to turn back now. It's time to die.

WRESTLING WITH GOD

When Jacob learned that Esau was coming, his first response was to pray. This was a smart move. His next moves, however, were less spiritual, and more fearful.

He started with bribes. He sent Esau more than five hundred animals (a fortune in those days) in separate droves, so that as Esau rode, he would encounter one gift after another.

> "For he thought, 'I may appease him with the present that goes ahead of me, and afterward I shall see his face. Perhaps he will accept me.'" (Genesis 32:20)

Hoping this would be enough, he went to bed. But he couldn't sleep. In "the same night," he arose and woke up his family. He sent his wives and children across the Jabbok ford along with all his possessions. It could be that he wanted them to run for safety. Maybe he thought that Esau would spare him if he saw the family first, and had the pick of Jacob's possessions. But I think he had something else in mind.

It says that "Jacob was left alone" (Genesis 32:24). Jacob has not been truly alone since he left Beersheba. Once in Haran, he had been surrounded by family and civilization. In the clamor of that crowd, he had perhaps been able to mute the cries of his conscience. Now, face to face with the possibility of seeing Esau again, Jacob revealed himself to be the same sniveling coward he had always been. He sent everyone and everything across the river. He was going to run for it.

But God had promised to always be with him. And you can't send God away like a drove of camels. In one of the most fascinating stories of the Bible, we read that "a man wrestled with [Jacob] until the breaking of the day" (Genesis 32:24). Hosea 12:4 will identify this "man" as an "angel," and a few verses later, in Genesis 32:30, it will say that Jacob has seen the face of God. In the night, all alone, scared out of his mind, Jacob turned to run back into the wilderness. But a man stopped him. This was no mere mortal, but the very Angel of the Lord: a divine, even Christological figure in the Old Testament. God had come to stop him.

Imagine the back-and-forth! Jacob trying to make his excuses while God insists that he face his brother. Jacob tried to run, but the angel tripped him. Jacob got mad and took a swing, then tried to run again – but the Lord tackled him to the ground. Don't picture this as a choreographed kung-fu battle, this was a *scrap*. Jacob was no fighter, but he was desperate, and he fought until the day began to dawn.

> "When the man saw that he did not prevail against Jacob, he touched his hip socket, and Jacob's hip was put out of joint as he wrestled with him." (Genesis 32:25)

As it became clear that Jacob was not going to give in, the Angel of the Lord popped his hip out of joint! This is UFC-level stuff right here. Jacob would have been screaming and writhing in pain. The fight is over. Jacob can no longer run even if he still wanted to.

Now what? He has nothing left. His brother will surely find him the next morning, crippled and helpless. It's too late to turn back. So Jacob does the only thing he can do: he grabs hold of the Lord and refuses to let go. The angel said to him,

> "'Let me go, for the day has broken.' But Jacob said, 'I will not let you go unless you bless me.'" (Genesis 32:26)

You must not think of Jacob putting God in a full nelson here. Jacob's hip was out of socket, all he can do is maybe grab the hem of His garment as He walks away. He was begging in the dirt.

Jacob finally acknowledged that he needed God's help. Every other time there had been a way for him to wriggle out, a scheme, a plan, a lie to move him forward. But now he had nothing left but God, and he knew that he couldn't make it on his own.

> "And [the Angel of the Lord] said to him, 'What is your name?' And he said, 'Jacob.' Then he said, 'Your name shall no longer be called Jacob, but Israel, for you have striven with God and with men, and have prevailed.'" (Genesis 32:27-28)

By asking him his name, the Lord was demanding that Jacob take full ownership of who he was and what he had done. Jacob! The Heel-Catcher, the trickster, the liar, the deceiver, the coward. He could not run from it anymore; this was rock bottom. He had no one and nothing, and his own identity was a shame to him.

But in a glorious act of forgiveness and mercy, God discarded Jacob's old identity and re-christened him, "Israel". We will discuss this name change in the next chapter. Jacob has finally made the turn that will lead him to his Promised Land. He has been welcomed into the purposes of God, and been given a new hope and a new future. He was blessed by the Lord, who did not reveal His own name – that would come later (Exodus 3:14).

In what was surely the worst night of his life, Jacob was literally beaten down by God and forced to do the right thing. But in that moment of breaking, he became willing to undergo the change that needed to take place. He passed through not just the waters of the Jordan River, but through the waters of death and rebirth by the grace of God.

PASSING THROUGH THE WATERS

I went to a Christian high school with weekly chapel services, so I have heard an awful lot of altar calls. I am sure you have heard one, when the preacher makes the offer of salvation or rededication. But have you ever heard the call to Christian conversion as a call to death? I have often heard it framed as a call to life, and it certainly is that, but it is equally a call to death.

From the very beginning of the world, God warned us that the penalty for sin was death. God told Adam as He placed him in the Garden of Eden,

"Of the tree of the knowledge of good and evil you shall not eat, for in the day that you eat of it you shall surely die." (Genesis 2:17)

Sound harsh? Let's put it this way: the moment you introduce evil and pain and suffering into God's perfect world, you are guilty of a capital crime. Ezekiel reiterated this point:

"The soul who sins shall die." (Ezekiel 18:20)

And in the New Testament:

"The wages of sin is death." (Romans 6:23)

This means the death of the body, but it also means the eternal death of the soul in Hell. A place, Jesus said, "where their worm does not die and the fire is not quenched" (Mark 9:48).

If that is the cosmic penalty for sin, then it makes perfect sense that the act of absolution, baptism for repentance, is a picture of death. It is an admission of guilt, an acceptance of justice. But many a criminal has gone to court with a great show of contrition, only for their sentence to be served anyway. It's not enough to be sorry, nor even to make restitution. The penalty must be carried out. And for us that means eternal death.

There is only one thing to be done. On the night of His arrest, Jesus prayed alone in the Garden of Gethsemane. He was in great distress, sweating and shaking. "My Father," He begged, "If it be possible, let this cup pass from me; nevertheless, not as I will, but as you will" (Matthew 26:39). Jesus wanted the "cup" to pass from Him if at all possible. This is the cup of God's wrath and judgment.

"For in the hand of the Lord there is a cup with foaming wine, well mixed, and he pours out from it, and all the wicked of the earth shall drain it down to the dregs." (Psalm 75:8)

Jesus was about to drink the cup of God's wrath in the place of those who deserved it.

Jesus Christ was the only one who did not deserve such death. He had never sinned. He was God in the flesh. And yet He willingly underwent the pain and indignity of crucifixion. He was betrayed by His friend with a kiss. Then arrested, beaten, and mocked by the soldiers. He endured humiliating unfair trials and was publicly shamed as a criminal. He was stripped and flogged with the vicious Roman cat o' nine tails. A crown of thorns was forced onto His head, blood streaming into His eyes. Finally, He was nailed hand and foot to the cross, where He died upon a hill called Calvary for all to see.

There is a beautiful song by Nichole Nordeman that asks a very simple question: Why? Why did Jesus have to die? Because the love of God is so great, even for miserable sinners like us, that He was willing to take judgment upon Himself so that He might pardon those who cry out for help. Jesus died as a sacrifice, as a perfect substitute. As the Son of Man He could shed His blood, but as the Son of God, His blood has wonder-working power to wash away every sin.

The way to be liberated from Hell is to have Christ's death count for you. Salvation, then, is identification with the death of Jesus. You must voluntarily embrace death, as He did. Baptism is the picture of burial in the likeness of His death and resurrection unto newness of life. Paul famously put it this way,

"I have been crucified with Christ. It is no longer I who live, but Christ who lives in me. And the life I now live in the flesh I live by faith in the Son of God, who loved me and gave himself for me." (Galatians 2:20)

The person who repents of their sins, believes in what Jesus has done on the cross, and cries out to God for mercy has identified with the death of Christ. And in that moment, a miraculous, spiritual work takes place. God applies the blood of Jesus to your life and your sins are taken away. You are counted righteous. God has forgiven your sins and justified you forever. The old you is dead, nailed to the cross with Jesus.

Then the Holy Spirit comes to you and takes up residence within your soul. You become a temple of God Himself. In an instant, your dead heart receives a charge of heavenly power, and starts to beat again. All the sickness of your soul is renewed by His presence, and you take your first breath of new life. The curse is taken away, the nightmare ends, and the new day begins.

It may not look as though anything has changed, but a difference has been wrought in you greater than any alteration to the body.

"If anyone is in Christ, he is a new creation. The old has passed away; behold, the new has come." (2 Corinthians 5:21)

You have died, and yet you live. You are alive for the first time. You have passed through the waters, and on the other side waits that abundant life, the destiny that God has prepared for you.

TAKE UP YOUR CROSS

That's a theological explanation of what it means to die to yourself. But if we cut through all of the doctrinal language, the action that must be taken is itself remarkably simple. There are many who have tripped over the simplicity of the Gospel and missed it. Paul summed it up nicely:

"If you confess with your mouth that Jesus is Lord and believe in your heart that God raised him from the dead, you will be saved." (Romans 10:9)

Is it really just as easy as believing the story of Jesus and asking for forgiveness? Well, it is certainly that simple, but I would not call it easy.

Let's look again at the example of Jacob. We could lay out his situation just as simply, if we like. All he needed to do was cross the river and talk to his brother. That's easy, right? So why did these simple steps terrify Jacob and cause him to flee? Why did God have to quite literally pin him down and make him do it? Because there is a difference between simple and easy. In crossing that river, he would be entirely out of his own control. Something deep in Jacob had to die, namely his self-reliance and cowardice. Such things do not go down without a fight.

I spoke of altar calls earlier. Looked at clinically, there is nothing simpler than getting out of your seat and kneeling at the front of a church, maybe saying a little prayer. But people will sweat and shake and weep and cry out in those moments. Seems like a lot of trouble for such a simple step, doesn't it? There is more going on here than meets the eye. There is a spiritual transformation taking place.

When my great-grandfather was saved, he got up and ran down the aisle as fast as he could when the invitation was given. He explained later that he was afraid he would die before he got the chance to pray the sinner's prayer. For him, that moment of conversion was life and death. He was as afraid in that moment as any soldier storming the beaches of Normandy. He was passing through the waters.

Grown, mature people do not have reactions like these to things that are light and easy. All that talk of dying with Christ is not just a metaphor, it is quite real. There is a death taking place in the spirit, as well as a rebirth. Repentance is a big part of it, but this is different than repentance. It's the difference between signing up for the Selective Service, and receiving a letter ordering you to Vietnam. Repentance is agreeing to life-saving surgery, regeneration is the operation itself with no anesthetic.

If you've made it this far in the book, you already know what needs to die in you. It is the flaw that caused all this trouble in the first place, it is the defining characteristic of the monster we met in the desert, it is the one thing that must be overcome to enter the Promised Land. This could be something minor, a weed that must be plucked before it grows too large. Or it could be something enormous, a tree whose roots are breaking up the concrete in your driveway. If you are not yet a believer, it could be as serious as your initial salvation.

But we are very often afraid to let go of the things that bind us. You've heard of Stockholm Syndrome, when prisoners develop love and loyalty for their captors. We all have Stockholm Syndrome to our sin. We can't imagine life without it! You might not like the fact that you cheat and steal to stay afloat financially, but you don't know any other way. You might hate the way you bully your kids, but you just don't think you could change. It could even be that you have defined yourself by your sin, privately and publicly. You call yourself loud, or alcoholic, or angry, or gay. These aren't things that you struggle against, they are things you have allowed to define you. You are comfortable in your sin, and the thought of never doing it again scares you.

Look again at what Jesus said about being His disciple:

199

"If anyone would come after me, let him deny himself and take up his cross and follow me. For whoever would save his life will lose it, but whoever loses his life for my sake will find it" (Matthew 16:24-25)

Jesus is calling you to imitate His actions on Mount Calvary. First, you must deny yourself. It does not matter how you were born, how you were raised, or what you have done since then. We are saying, "No!" to all of it, as an entirety. You can bring nothing with you across the Jordan, you must renounce it all.

Second, you must take up your cross. People who carry crosses end up dead. You must allow God to put you to death. Your soul must pass through the waters and drown. When you make this commitment, there is no going back. The old life must die, so you'd better let it go if you want to move forward.

And third, you must follow Him. Jesus Christ can teach you how to live. He will give you His Holy Spirit to help you, if you will let Him. It will be different and unfamiliar from anything you've done before, but it will be wonderful. The cost of admission to the Promised Land is everything you have and everything you are.

BAPTISM BY WATER AND FIRE

The image of passing through the waters is used throughout the Bible as a symbol of death and rebirth. Baptism is the primary illustration, the Christian initiatory rite. But even that is calling back to other examples from Scripture. Creation itself is described as God bringing forth the world out of "the deep...the face of the waters" (Genesis 1:2). Old Testament poets would describe their deliverance as the defeat of a great sea serpent when they passed through the depths (Job 26:12, Psalm 89:10).

The best example is when Israel passed through the waters of the Red Sea in the book of Exodus. God parted the sea and they passed through on dry ground while Pharaoh's armies were drowned as the waters collapsed. Jesus would reenact this story at His baptism when He went under the water and out into the wilderness. Likewise, we must allow our oppressive sins to die as we move forward into a new life with Christ.

But there is another story about Israel and the waters that we must not forget. After crossing the Red Sea, God brought them to Mount Sinai, where He established a Covenant with them and gave them His Law. From there, God led them to the boundaries of Canaan at Kadesh-barnea. All that was left was for them to enter the Land and take hold of it. But when their scouts returned, they warned the people that the inhabitants of the land were giants, and that they would be crushed if they attempted the crossing. The people panicked and refused to go in, voting instead to kill Moses and return to Egypt. Only God's timely intervention prevented this catastrophe.

For their rebellion, God doomed them to wander in the wilderness for forty years, until that cowardly generation had died off. Only Caleb and Joshua, the two faithful spies, would live to see what their brothers had refused. Israel's unwillingness to let go of the security of slavery kept them from experiencing the land of milk and honey. But they could not go back. They wandered until they were old and bent, and then dead and gone.

But when Joshua led the people to the river the second time, they saw a repeat of the Red Sea. The priests entered the water first, carrying the Ark of the Covenant. As they got halfway through the floodwaters, the flow stopped, and the people crossed over on dry ground. Those who had the faith to face the certainty of death were rewarded with the promises that had been intended for them all along. But those who refused to accept the loss of what they already had, received nothing.

Dying to yourself is a lifelong process, a daily discipline. But very often we have key moments when we must let go of our lives in order to gain what God has for us. Daniel was one such person. His opponents could find no dirt on him to accuse him, so they outlawed prayer. Daniel could have taken the easy way out, but instead he continued in obedience to the Lord. He was arrested and thrown to the lions, but you know the story. God preserved him through the night. He passed through, not the waters exactly, but through the shadow of death, and emerged unscathed. A dreadful night, no doubt, but it was all worth it.

His companions, Hananiah, Mishael and Azariah (also known as Shadrach, Meshach and Abednego), were also willing to face death for what was right. They refused to bow down and worship the king's golden image, and for that they were thrown into the fiery furnace. Yet Nebuchadnezzar saw a fourth man in the fire, shining like the sun. God was with them, and they emerged not even smelling like smoke. They passed the test. They did not count their lives dear to themselves but were willing to give up their lives in obedience to God.

The Lord said through the prophet Isaiah,

"When you pass through the waters, I will be with you; and through the rivers, they shall not overwhelm you; when you walk through fire you shall not be burned, and the flame shall not consume you." (Isaiah 43:2)

As terrified as you may be to cross that river, to face that pit or fiery furnace, you truly have nothing to fear. The only thing that burned in that furnace were the ropes that bound Shadrach and his companions. God will be with you, and you will come out the other side to the Promised Land you have been searching for. Don't let the Devil scare you into turning back.

TAP OUT

The image of Jacob wrestling with God is certainly a fitting one. Of course, this isn't like *God of War*, or *Clash of the Titans*. You wouldn't stand any more of a chance than Jacob did in a fight like that. It's a spiritual struggle. You probably feel like you're wrestling with God right now. Every argument against total surrender to Jesus has reared up, the arguments for submission seem flimsy while your flesh throws a temper tantrum. This is the moment of truth, the final battle, the decision that will determine your future forever.

There's a great MMA flick called *Warrior*. It's like a modern-day *Rocky*, starring Joel Edgerton, Tom Hardy and Nick Nolte. Nolte plays a reformed alcoholic father whose two sons want nothing to do with him. Brennan, played by Edgerton, has made a good life for himself, getting married and having children, although his teacher's salary is slowly dragging him down. Hardy plays Tommy, the angry, bitter brother estranged from them both. The brothers enter a mixed martial-arts competition and end up facing each other down in the final match. Their fight becomes a metaphor for Tommy's unwillingness to open up and let his brother and father love him. At the end of the second round, Brennan seriously injures his brother, but Tommy refuses to throw in the towel. A tearful Brennan grapples Tommy to the ground as their father watches.

"Tap, Tommy," he begs. "It's okay. It's okay. I love you."

And in that moment, Tommy taps out of the fight. But there's a bigger picture. He has given up fighting and raging against the world and is willing to accept the love of his family.

In Hosea 12:4, the prophet describes Jacob's struggle against the Lord. "He strove with the angel and prevailed" – wait a minute, didn't Jacob lose? Didn't he get his hip knocked out of joint and gain a limp for the rest of his life? Yes, he did. But he still won. How is that? "He wept and sought his favor." That was how Jacob won. He tapped out. He begged God to take him on that final journey through the waters. He died to himself, and he gained new life forever.

It's time for you to tap out. You've been wrestling with God for too long now. You know what you've got to do, but you've been avoiding it. There's a pit in your heart into which you don't dare to look. It paralyzes you. You might even read books like this one hoping to salve the sting. But that won't work for you anymore. It hasn't worked up till now.

It's okay. The Lord is going to be there to catch you. He needs to break you, because that old self needs to die. You might not know what is waiting on the other side. But put your trust in the love of Jesus and His Father and the Holy Spirit who will come to guide you through. You've been struggling long enough. It's time to surrender.

STUDY QUESTIONS

1.) What has God been trying to teach you through this book? Are you prepared to take the final step?

2.) Are we incapable of saving ourselves? Why must we die to live anew in Christ? Why do we need God to accomplish this?

3.) Do you think Jacob was going to run away? If not, why do you think God wrestled with him at the brook? How do you picture this scene in your mind?

4.) Does it surprise you that God would permanently cripple Jacob? Has God ever broken you for your own good?

5.) What was the cup that Jesus was so afraid to drink (Matthew 26:39, Psalm 75:8)? Why did He go through with it?

6.) "If anyone is in Christ, he is a new creation. The old has passed away; behold, the new has come." (2 Corinthians 5:21) If knew this was true, how might it change your life?

7.) Why are altar calls so emotional for people, even if they are so simple? Have you ever had an emotional moment of repentance?

8.) Jesus told us to deny ourselves and take up our crosses (Matthew 16:24-25). How is this different from the message we usually hear from the world? What would this look like for you?

9.) The "waters" provide a strong symbol in the Bible. Israel passed through the waters twice, Christians engage in baptism. What does this symbol mean for the process of spiritual growth?

10.) Why does victory over God involve "tapping out," or surrendering? Is there anything you are scared to surrender to God?

11

A NEW NAME

JACOB BECOMES ISRAEL

(Genesis 32:27-32)

BORN AGAIN

These days there are two different terms used to describe a change in worldview. Each is associated with one side of the political divide. If you are on the Left, you speak about being "woke." You have awakened to the way the world really is, and can recognize all of its injustices. Those on the Right speak about being "red-pilled". This is a reference to *The Matrix,* in which Neo takes a red pill that allows him to see that all the world is a computer simulation. Many feel they have been lied to by the media or higher education, and now they can see the truth. Both of these terms mean essentially the same thing – and they are both pretty cringy!

As Christians, we have our own time-honored description of personal transformation. It comes from the words of Jesus to a man named Nicodemus, who was a teacher and ruler of the Jews. Jesus told him,

"Truly, truly, I say to you, unless one is born again he cannot see the kingdom of God." (John 3:3)

Nicodemus was confused, but Jesus explained that this was "of water and the Spirit" (John 3:5). Lefties are woke, righties are red-pilled, but Christians have been born again.

The last chapter spoke of the sobering need to die to yourself. It's a hard process, but we should not become preoccupied with momentary pain. Women endure childbirth, said to be the worst pain a person can endure. And yet they immediately enthuse that it was worth it, and sometimes even go back for seconds! This is what happens when we arrive on the other side of the Jordan. We find ourselves born anew of water (remember our references to passing "through the waters") and the Holy Spirit.

Jacob was not just broken by God, he was given new life by God. He was given a new purpose, a new home and a new name. Jesus died and rose from the dead to give us the chance to be born again. He wants to take all the corrupted pieces of our lives and recalibrate them to spread love instead of further pain.

You will never be the same after you have passed through the waters. That's an intimidating thing. But you will pass *through*. On the other side, everything will take on new meaning. As we are now, we cannot inherit the Kingdom that awaits us across the river, but if we are born again, then we are fit to inhabit the Promised Land.

Being woke or red-pilled is to recognize the supposed hidden truth about the world. Being born again will allow you to see the world by the corrective lens of the Holy Spirit, and there will be much for you to do afterwards. But this change is superior to all others because it represents not just a change of mind or opinion, but a fundamental transformation of the heart.

ISRAEL

There lied Jacob, exhausted, afraid and broken. His hip was out of joint, and his leg seared with pain. As the sun's first rays broke over the horizon, the Angel of the Lord turned to go. Jacob lunged for Him, only able to grab the hem of His robe. His muscles were weak and the pain was unbearable, but he held on. The Lord told him to let go, but he vowed to hold on until he was blessed.

The Angel said to him, "What is your name?" Jacob no doubt felt the full weight of that sentence. The Lord knew good and well who he was, but this was a symbolic question. It meant: What defines you? Who are you as a person? In the depths of your soul, who are you, really? With his eyes cast down and his voice thick with tears, he replied, "Jacob" (Genesis 32:27).

In that name was bound up the story of his life so far. Jacob, Heel-Catcher, the one who cheats to get ahead, the one afraid to speak forthrightly, the pushover, the sneak, the liar. It echoed into his past as he set a pattern of passivity and manipulation in his youth. It spoke of the fateful day when he allowed his mother to cajole him into deception and theft. It carried with it the long miles in the wilderness, and the bittersweet arrival at Laban's house. The betrayal by his uncle was there, as were decades of abuse in his house. He remembered his attempts to catch Laban's heel by selectively breeding the flocks. There was the frustration that caused him to leave, and the fear that almost cost him everything. And just the night before, he had tried to escape with bribes and schemes and even thought of running away. All of that was bound up in a word: Jacob. But God said to him,

> "Your name shall no longer be Jacob, but Israel, for you have striven with God and with men, and have prevailed." (Genesis 32:28)

In a surprising act of sovereign grace, God chose to accept Jacob's humble cry for help and redeem his broken life. In this moment, although none of the dangers had passed away, Jacob received what he had been looking for all along. No longer was he the Heel-Catcher. Now he was *Yisrael*.

Israel comes from the word *El*, meaning "God" and *yasar*, meaning "to contend or struggle". That is a fitting description of Jacob, is it not? He had struggled with men, most of all Laban, and he had indeed come out on top. And he had struggled with God, not just the night before, but his whole life. Had he prevailed against God? Put it this way – he had found the way to victory in a struggle with God, which is to surrender. He had fought the battle to its conclusion and would receive his share of the spoils. He was now to be known as the one who struggles with or for God. Isn't that a much better spin on Jacob's tenacity than Heel-Catcher?

Instead of a cheat and a liar, God named him one who meets the enemy face to face. Instead of a passive observer, God named him a contender in the ring. Instead of a burr under the saddle of the world, God named him the man who would never give up. God had taken the worst qualities of Jacob and not destroyed them, but redirected them in the right direction. He was the same man, and yet he would never be the same.

That name would come to define not just Jacob himself, but all of his descendants. Over and over again the Bible will refer to the children of Israel. Not of Isaac, not even of Abraham, but Israel. This man, for all his shortcomings, had fought the fight and tapped out at the right moment. He was ready to receive the blessing and to pass it on to his children.

Jacob asked him, "Please tell me your name," but in an Aslan-like moment, the Angel simply said, "Why is it that you ask my name?" (Genesis 32:29). Jacob named the place of his crossing Peniel (or Penuel), which means, "Face of God." And as he passed into Canaan at long last, the sun rose upon him, "limping because of his hip" (Genesis 32:31). It had not been an easy journey. He would carry that scar the rest of his life. But this was no longer Jacob the cowardly deceiver. This was Israel – he who contends even with God.

THE LATTER GLORY

In 586 B.C., Babylon sacked the city of Jerusalem, destroyed the Temple and scattered the people. It was the single greatest blow to the Jewish cultural consciousness up to that time. For seventy years the people languished in Exile, waiting for the day prophesied by Jeremiah when they could return to their homeland.

The book of Ezra narrates that joyful return. A handful of faithful Hebrews, all of whose names are recorded as a testimony to their faith, traveled back to Jerusalem to rebuild the city and the Temple. Under the leadership of Zerubbabel the governor and Joshua the high priest, they got to work. Two years and two months after their arrival, the foundation of the new Temple was laid. The people gathered for a great celebration, with loud singing. However, there was a problem.

"Many of the priests and Levites and heads of fathers' houses, old men who had seen the first house, wept with a loud voice when they saw the foundation of this house being laid, though many shouted for joy, so that the people could not distinguish the sound of the joyful shout from the sound of the people's weeping, for the people shouted with a great shout, and the sound was heard far away." (Ezra 3:12-13)

At the great reveal of the Temple foundation, the noise was incredible. The younger generation was ecstatic, and shouted for joy at the realization of all their hopes. But the old timers, who had seen the masterwork that was Solomon's Temple, were not impressed. They could tell its inferiority just by looking at the foundation. They wept with a loud voice, mingling with the celebration and no doubt tarnishing the moment for those who had worked on it.

The simple truth was that these men and women were not as capable as their ancestors. These were not the best craftsmen that Israel had to offer, they were all back in Babylon. These were those who had answered the call, and they had done their best. But their best was not very good. Over time the infectious despair of the grandfathers among them began to poison the enthusiasm of the people.

But God had a different view of all this. He sent the prophet Haggai to say,

"Who is left among you who saw this house in its former glory? How do you see it now? Is it not as nothing in your eyes?" (Haggai 2:3)

God didn't shy away from the truth. But neither did He allow the people to stew in their discouragement. He told their leaders,

Zerubbabel and Joshua to "be strong." "Work," He told them, "for I am with you...my Spirit remains in your midst" (Haggai 2:4-5). God told them to keep going, even though He knew that they could only produce an inferior product. The only thing that mattered to God was their obedience and their faith. And through Haggai, He made them an incredible promise:

> "The latter glory of this house shall be greater than the former." (Haggai 2:9)

The people took heart and finished the Temple. It was unimpressive, but it was the house of the Lord. Over the years, there would be a wealth of history and testimony attached to that Temple. It was there that Antiochus Epiphanes placed an idol of Zeus and sacrificed a pig in the Holy Place. When the people rose up and cast off the yoke of Greece, it was in this Temple that God made the oil for the lamp last for eight days – the traditional story of Hanukkah. Eventually, Herod the Great would renovate this Temple and make it a glorious piece of architecture again. It was at this Temple that the priests took a stand against Pontius Pilate by refusing to allow Roman graven images. It was this Temple that would be cleansed by Jesus Christ Himself. Here would echo the words, "Render to Caesar the things that are Caesar's" (Matthew 22:21), and it was the veil of this Temple that was rent in two. This Temple's gate called Beautiful would witness the miracle of a lame man walking, and it was in this Temple that the early Church would meet by the thousands. James would be thrown from the pinnacle of this Temple, Paul would preach the Gospel there from the steps of the Roman Antonia fortress, and it was this Temple that was destroyed in fulfillment of the words of Jesus. As wonderful as the times of David and Solomon and Josiah might have been, the latter glory was indeed greater than the former.

This is what we call redemption. To redeem something means to buy it back, to purchase it again. When we are born again, we are what the Bible calls "infants in Christ" (1 Corinthians 3:1). Our souls have been changed, but we are still weak in a lot of ways. We're still in the same circumstances, we have the same habits, and there is a long way to go before we arrive at our final destination. It is tempting to be discouraged in those moments. The lofty plans of God sound impossible, or even ridiculous. The Devil whispers that we will never be good enough, because we are still in the same old mess. But as the Lord said through Zechariah in the same situation,

"Whoever has despised the day of small things shall rejoice." (Zechariah 4:10)

God is not worried by a lack of early progress.

"The silver is mine, and the gold is mine, declares the Lord of hosts." (Haggai 2:8)

God makes it His business to bring about the destiny He has planned. And He is so confident of that coming glory that He redeems us. He buys us back from sin and gives us a new name. We may not be there yet, but God is not in a hurry. His eyes are on the latter glory. "Behold," He says from Heaven, "I am making all things new" (Revelation 21:5).

THE BEST VERSION OF YOU

Names are interesting things. Different cultures have different preferences, with their own trends and cycles. Right now, the American trend is to use last names as first names. My sons play baseball, and it can be hard to find a Jimmy or a Johnny on one of their teams. But names like Knox or Reynolds or Fisher are commonplace. These days, we mostly just pick names that we think sound good (even if we have to invent them!). My wife and I gave our children each a family name and a name of our choosing, but there is no real standard practice for how to name kids anymore.

In the Bible, names were much more significant. Names were considered to be prophetic, and many were exactly that. Samuel means "God Hears," because the barren Hannah was granted a child from the Lord when she prayed. Ichabod's name meant "No Glory," because he was born the day the Ark of the Covenant was stolen from Israel. Hosea had three children, Jezreel, Lo-Ammi and Lo-Ruhamah, that all had prophetic names. It was not uncommon for a name to change later on to something more descriptive. Consider how Esau took on the name Edom, because of his ruddy appearance.

So when God changed Jacob's name, it was a watershed moment in his life. That's what being born again is, a moment when the flow of your life totally changes. But by giving Jacob his new name, God was also giving a prophecy. Jacob had undergone a change, but he would still need many years before he could live it out to the fullest. His descendants would need longer still. It was an act of hope on the part of God, His willingness to anticipate the latter glory.

This new name then, Israel, was descriptive of who Jacob could become if he would fully live out the destiny that God had planned for him. It is different and yet similar to his old name. *Yacov* meant "Heel-

Catcher," as you know, the trickster, the deceiver. But *Yisrael* meant "Contends With God," the contender, the one willing to struggle to the end. It indicates a relationship with God. One name describes passive, backdoor dealings, and the other straightforward, manly conduct.

And yet they are quite similar. Both describe contention of some kind, and both describe a competitive attitude. God was not turning Jacob into a completely different person. He was redeeming the person that he already was. God took the best qualities of Jacob, removed the sin from them, and aimed them in the right direction. His drive to do well, his persistence and endurance, and his savor for the struggle, were all redeemed and put to good use for the Kingdom of God.

When you submit to the Lord, He will give you a new name. He will take the best parts of you and redeem them. He will draw out your true identity apart from the sin that has corrupted it. All of the noble qualities that have been twisted into sin will shine through for all to see. What might God make out of you?

Maybe you are a driven, ambitious person. You are prone to workaholism, and you neglect your family and your health. That's not good, but what if God renames and redeems you? You'll lose the obsession and the neglect, but keep the willingness to work hard and do your best. Such people are great assets to those around them; their accomplishments benefit everyone else.

Maybe you are controlling and manipulative. You twist your kids' arms with guilt and you nag your spouse into doing what you want. God wants to rename and redeem you. At the root of all that is a true love for your family, you just don't know how to show it. God wants to turn that love into a healthy, thriving heartbeat that everyone can depend upon.

Maybe you are arrogant about your intelligence. You talk down to people, you withdraw from your community, and you are convinced that no one is smarter than you. But all that gets renamed and redeemed when you cross the Jordan. God can still use those smarts. But now you're not hoarding knowledge for its own sake, you're learning with a purpose. You become a teacher or a scholar or an apologist. Rather than seeing facts as trophies, you enjoy the pleasure of learning for its own sake without the need to puff yourself up.

The examples go on and on! Rock stars are redeemed to write amazing songs for the Church. Wife beaters become defenders of the weak. Bitter activists become mighty evangelists. Our churches are full of these testimonies. Anyone who argues that Jesus doesn't change lives is simply ignorant. God is redeeming new people every day. And those early steps are often ugly, but God loves to bestow new names on people with prophetic significance. He sees what can be, and His greatest joy is to make those plans reality.

When you lose your life in Christ, you find it for the first time. Jesus is not looking to fundamentally change who you are – He is trying to *show* you who you fundamentally are. Satan has deceived you into thinking that you are defined by your sin. Jesus wants to show you who you could be without all that nonsense. He wants to redeem you. He wants to draw out the best possible version of you by the power of His Holy Spirit. You might think you know your name, but Jesus has a better one waiting for you.

B.C. AND A.D.

Many of God's greatest heroes received a new name at a pivotal point of their life. It's similar to how we divide history between B.C. (Before Christ), and A.D. (*Anno Domini*, "Year of Our Lord"). Of course, now scholars prefer to use B.C.E. (Before Common Era) and C.E. (Common Era) – a silly piece of P.C. in my opinion. But however you label it, we're still dividing history by the life of Jesus! And that's how our lives are divided as well.

The first example is Abraham. At first, his name was Abram, which means "Exalted Father". Over time, this name became embarrassing for him, since he was the father of exactly nobody. But when Abram was 90, God renamed him. You might think God would give him a less demeaning moniker, but instead God doubled down.

> "No longer shall your name be called Abram, but your name shall be Abraham, for I have made you the father of a multitude of nations." (Genesis 17:5)

From "Exalted Father", he was now to be called "Father of a Multitude". This would have been extra embarrassing! But it was God's way of assuring him of His promise. And of course we now know that Father Abraham did indeed have many sons.

Let's talk about Simon Peter. His name was Simon, a very common name at this time, given for one of the twelve Hebrew tribes. But Jesus gave Simon a new name.

> "And I tell you, you are Peter, and on this rock I will build my church, and the gates of hell shall not prevail against it." (Matthew 16:18)

Peter means "Rock". And Peter was kind of a hardheaded guy, wasn't he? He was stubborn, he was belligerent, and he was not afraid to let his opinions be known. We see that and we laugh or cringe. But

Jesus saw him as the kind of person He could use to build His Church. The Apostles needed to be men who would be stubborn in the face of opposition and insist upon the truth. God took those qualities of Simon, filled him with the Spirit, and then turned him loose as Peter.

Another great example is that of Paul. He was born as Saul of Tarsus, named for the first king of Israel. It was a strong, noble name. And Saul was a strong, noble guy. He studied under Gamaliel and caught the attention of the Jewish rulers. He was eventually allowed to hunt down Christians for them, so zealous was he for the Law. No doubt the early Church prayed that God would strike him down. But the Lord saw Saul's zeal and intellect and courage and could only see how wonderful it would be if only he were redeemed. So God reached out to save him. And starting in Acts 13:9, he was known as Paul, a name that simply means "Small". God took all the things Saul was and redeemed them for His glory.

One other example is John the son of Zebedee, the youngest of the disciples. John's writings are unique because he does not like to name himself. In his Gospel he refers to himself as "The Disciple Whom Jesus Loved". In his letters he calls himself simply "The Elder". Only in Revelation does he give his own name. For him, his own reputation was of little significance.

But there was another name given to John. He and his brother James were nicknamed by Jesus, *Boanerges*, which means "Sons of Thunder". Once, when a city in Samaria refused to give them lodging, they asked Jesus for permission to call down fire from Heaven (Luke 9:54)! We might see that heart and look for somebody else. But God knew He could use that fire. There's a story from Church history in which John the Apostle took a liking to a young disciple. But the young man fell away, and became the leader of a dangerous band of robbers.

When he heard it, John went straight to their hideout and demanded to see him. The man saw he was there and ran away, ashamed. But John chased him down, shouting for him to repent, which eventually he did! Who else but a Son of Thunder would be willing to do that?

WRITTEN ON A WHITE STONE

When you were born, you were given a name. Your parents picked it out for you and wrote it down on the birth certificate application after a lot of planning and arguing and thought. When you are born again, your heavenly Father has a new name waiting for you as well. Sometimes we get a name that we don't much care for, or that doesn't fit us very well. But that's never true with your new name. God knows you better than you know yourself. Your new name is not a projection of somebody else's expectations, but a redemption of all of the best parts of you.

God-given names are prophetic. He knows that you're not there yet. It's always wonderful and miraculous when old sins are done away with in an instant, but most of the time we have a long road of discipline and struggle ahead of us. That was the case for Jacob. It was the case for Peter. And it could be the case for you. You might even be in prison, or some other situation that has no chance of changing. But God doesn't want you to worry about that. He wants you to keep your eyes on the latter glory. What you *will be* is what gets God excited, not your present inadequacies.

Maybe you have been told you are worthless or a mistake. Parents and spouses and teachers can say terrible things that cause us to view ourselves as damaged. But no one is irredeemable. Hosea's three children were given tragic names that spoke of their shameful births. But God changed them from names of cursing to names of blessing

(Hosea 2:23). He told Israel that He would give them a new name: no longer "Desolate," but, "My Delight Is In Her" (Isaiah 62:2-4). Your new name speaks of God's love and plans for you. That's why so many Christians from idolatrous cultures change their names when they are saved. They want to testify to the living and loving God who saved their soul.

Consider what God might do through you if He got ahold of those parts of you that lie unused. Your talents and skills, your resources and personality, your strengths and even your weaknesses. All of that can be redeemed and renamed. That's true abundant life right there, the best version of yourself firing on all cylinders with no corruption and no guilt. God said of mankind as they built the Tower of Babel, "Nothing that they propose to do will now be impossible for them" (Genesis 11:6). If that was true of sinners in rebellion against God, how much more a born-again man of God alive with the power of the Holy Spirit?

In Heaven, the Bible says we will all be given new names.

> "To the one who conquers I will give...a white stone, with a new name written on the stone that no one knows except the one who receives it." (Revelation 2:17)

Not just a new name, but a secret name. Because only God and you will ever know the depths of all that He has done for you. That name has already been written, your destiny decided. And if you are born again, a new christening has already taken place.

STUDY QUESTIONS

1.) Read the story of Nicodemus in John 3. What does it mean to be "born again"? Have you been born again?

2.) Being "woke" or "red-pilled" means to recognize unseen truths about the world. What truths do we learn when we are born again? What responsibility do we have after this?

3.) Can you see how God redeemed Jacob's old life? How was the name "Israel" the positive redemption of the old "Jacob"?

4.) Have you been discouraged by your early efforts at spiritual growth? Did you give up? How should you have handled it?

5.) How does it feel to know that God is focused on making things new instead of dredging up the past? Do you focus on the past too much?

6.) Read Hosea 1-3 to learn the story of Hosea's children. What did their names mean? What did God promise to do about those names in Hosea 2:21-23?

7.) What parts of your personality could God redeem? How would those qualities look after they are redeemed?

8.) Jesus chose a lot of hotheaded young men to be His disciples. What qualities in those men were useful after the Spirit had come upon them? What does that tell us about God's perspective?

9.) Have you ever been told that you are worthless? Did you believe it at the time? Do you believe it now? Do you know that God loves you with an everlasting love?

10.) Does it excite you to think that you have a new name awaiting you in Heaven? How ought you to live from now on if this is true?

12

THE REST IS UP TO YOU

JACOB IS REUNITED WITH ESAU

(Genesis 33)

YOU ARE THE SOLUTION

I don't know that I had a moment when I transitioned from boyhood to manhood. There were certainly a number of mile markers: my wedding, the birth of my first child, my ordination or graduation. But to me, adulthood is something that you realize has already happened to you. You wake up one day and know that the grown-ups are not coming to help you – you are the grown-up now.

That sense of responsibility is needed to live the life that God has assigned to you. You can't wait for your mother or your grandfather or your pastor to live it for you. It's you and God, and no one else. Many of us try to put as much of our lives out of our hands as possible through habits and structure. But you can organize your life as much as you like, it all boils down to you doing the right thing. And that can be a frightful prospect.

I've seen this in recent days in the Church. Great men like Billy Graham and Chuck Smith and Jerry Falwell have passed from the scene leaving – us. And who are we to follow in the footsteps of giants like that? It's like the death of Gandalf or Dumbledore or Obi-Wan Kenobi. He was the one who knew the way, he was the one with the plan. But the quest must go on, as must your life.

But here's the tremendous truth. If you step out in the steps that God has laid out before you, you will find that you are more capable than you ever imagined. When you realize that only the strength of God counts, you realize that you are as powerful as any hero of the faith, because you have access to the same power. Paul wrote that God is "able to do far more abundantly than all that we ask or think." We all believe that. But finish the sentence: "according to the power at work within us" (Ephesians 3:20)! God's power is released through your life. The weight of the world is on your shoulders, but if you have been on your journey to the wilderness, God has given you the strength to bear it.

You are the solution the world is waiting for. Creation itself is groaning for the revelation of the sons of God (Romans 8:19). Your family needs you, your city needs you, your country needs you. At first you will be scared by your own inadequacy. Then you will be astonished at God's mighty power. And then you will be victorious.

In C.S. Lewis's space novel, *Perelandra*, the main character, Ransom, is charged with protecting a new Eden on Venus from the intrusion of the Devil. It's a fascinating parable, and it teaches a great lesson. Ransom knows he must stop Satan from tempting that planet's version of Eve, but he doesn't know what to do. He argues and argues with him, but is unable to make any headway. He begs for God to step in and save the girl. But he comes to understand that *he* is the help that God has sent. And as mundane as it seems, he will have to battle the evil one himself. He slays the wicked avatar, saving all of Perelandra in so doing.

You are the solution. You've prayed and you've waited, but now it's time to live out your destiny. You're ready.

REUNION, RESTORATION, REVIVAL

Jacob limped across the brook as morning came.

"And behold, Esau was coming, and four hundred men with him." (Genesis 33:1)

This was the moment of truth. Everything he had been dreading was coming true. But things were different now. This was not Jacob anymore, this was Israel. He had wrestled with God and man, and he was returning to Canaan with a new heart.

He organized the children with their mothers, but this time he did not send them ahead to buffer his escape.

"He himself went on before them, bowing himself to the ground seven times, until he came near to his brother." (Genesis 33:3)

No more running, he was stepping out to meet his brother in great humility. He was, after all, the one who had wronged Esau. Whatever retribution his brother was going to bring, he was prepared to face it.

"But Esau ran to meet him and embraced him and fell on his neck and kissed him, and they wept." (Genesis 33:4)

What an unexpected twist! Jacob believed that Esau had ridden out to make good on his deadly promise. And in all honesty, that's probably what Esau had done. But when he saw his twin brother coming to meet him, not full of pride, but humble and repentant, with gifts and kind words, his hard heart broke. In an instant they were boys again, and all the pain of the last twenty years fell away as they embraced.

Esau was delighted to meet his sisters-in-law and his niece and nephews. Introductions were given, but then Esau said, "What do you mean by all this company that I met?" That would be the gifts of animals that Jacob sent ahead.

"Jacob answered, 'To find favor in the sight of my lord.' But Esau said, 'I have enough, my brother; keep what you have for yourself.' Jacob said, 'No, please, if I have found favor in your sight, then accept my present from my hand. For I have seen your face, which is like seeing the face of God, and you have accepted me. Please accept my blessing that is brought to you, because God has dealt graciously with me, and because I have enough.'" (Genesis 33:8-11)

Who are these guys? Could this possibly be the same feuding twins from before? The blowhard and the trickster? By his humility and his graciousness, Jacob has won the heart of Esau. No longer is the warlord of Edom spoiling for a fight, he is just glad to have his brother back. Jacob has brought peace to his family.

Esau invited Jacob to come to Seir, but Jacob declined. He insisted that he would come later, but his family could not stand the long journey just now. Plus, he probably knew that while things may have been patched up, there was no need to push it. So the brothers parted for a time, at peace at last. The nations that descended from them would often be at each other's throats and go to war with one another frequently. But there were no other conflicts between Esau and Jacob in the Bible.

Jacob moved into the Promised Land, where he belonged. He lived at Succoth and then Shechem, where he purchased his first piece of property in Canaan. This is a significant moment – the carrier of the Promise has come home. And in that place, "he erected an altar and called it El-Elohe-Israel" (Genesis 33:20), which means "God, the God of Israel". He had met God in the wilderness, and now he introduced Him to his family.

Now, of course, Jacob had a lot of life left to live after this, and he had many other adventures. He didn't always get it right, but he walked with God from that day forward. He made good on his promise to worship God at Bethel, he led his family in the destruction of their idols, and he was reunited with his father before his death. Was everything perfect? No. But it was better. Jacob did that. Rather, God did that through Jacob. And when he died in Egypt, he was given a state funeral, and his bones were carried back to the land that would bear his name and laid alongside his fathers, Abraham and Isaac (Genesis 50:13). It had been a long journey, but he had done his part to hold the family together, to carry the Promise, and pass it on to his children. He was ready to take his rightful place at their side.

THIS LITTLE LIGHT OF MINE

If you grew up in church, then you have a repertoire of songs in your memory that can never be eradicated. This is true of men and women of all different denominations, backgrounds and income brackets. Classics like "Deep and Wide", "Father Abraham" and "Jesus Loves Me". If your church was a little more edgy, you might even know the infamous "Cartoon Song" by Chris Rice. These songs often come out of important sections of Scripture to aid in memorization and understanding. We're going to use one such song as an illustration right now.

"This little light of mine, I'm gonna let it shine!" You know this one, I'm sure. We are to let our light shine. We are to "Let it shine till Jesus comes," never to "let Satan *poof* it out," and shall we "hide it under a bushel? No! I'm gonna let it shine".

I remember a commercial for some baby product using this song. It crooned that we should let the children shine like stars. But this is not just some sappy platitude. It comes from Jesus' Sermon on the Mount:

> "You are the salt of the earth, but if salt has lost its taste, how shall its saltiness be restored? It is no longer good for anything except to be thrown out and trampled under people's feet. You are the light of the world. A city set on a hill cannot be hidden. Nor do people light a lamp and put it under a basket, but on a stand, and it gives light to all in the house. In the same way, let your light shine before others, so that they may see your good works and give glory to your Father who is in heaven." (Matthew 5:13-16)

Salt and light. That's what Jesus said we are. We ought to let our light shine, little as it may be. As of this writing, there are no great kids' songs about being salty. But both of these things combine to tell us that we are not just transformed for our own sake. God doesn't just make good people, nor does He just fix individual situations. He lights lamps in the darkness that dispel the gloom as long as they shine.

Let's break this passage down. First, Jesus says we are the salt of the earth. And that the purpose of salt is ruined when it loses its saltiness. What does this mean? Salt enhances flavor. If you can taste the salt, then there's too much. Salt is intended to draw out the flavor that is already in the meal. And that is what we do once we have been born again. We enhance life. Jesus came to give us abundant life (John 10:10). When you are filled with God's purpose and sent out in His power, you make life better for those around you: marriages, jobs, churches, schools. We are the salt of the earth.

And we are the light of the world. This is a lofty title, because Jesus Himself claimed to be the light of the world (John 8:12). But by the Holy Spirit, He has multiplied Himself millions of times over to shine His light. The light of truth, the light of hope, the light of peace and kindness and forgiveness and so much more. If you are living in His light, it cannot be hidden. You don't put a basket over your lamp (that's a much better translation, by the way, I had no clue what a bushel was when I was a kid!), but you set it out to help everyone else.

You have experienced the light of the world in your own life. It changed you. It healed you. It brought restoration to your life. Don't keep that to yourself. You *can't* keep it to yourself. People will sit up and notice. They'll wonder why you are so happy, or why your kids don't fight with you, or why you don't speak with filthy language. In that moment, we are to shine the light and let them know that the

231

secret is not us. The secret is Christ Himself and His work on the cross. As Chuck Smith said, grace changes everything. And people are looking to be changed. We've got to shine that light.

But there's a corollary. No one shone the light brighter than Jesus Himself, and they nailed Him to the cross. The light is a reproach to those who are living in darkness. It calls them higher and exposes their own guilt. Many would rather extinguish it. There's a scene in *A Christmas Carol* when Ebenezer Scrooge tries to douse the light of the Ghost of Christmas Past by pressing his cap down on his head. But the light shines out from under it anyway, because he cannot escape his memories. The same is true of the Gospel on a far greater scale:

> "This is the judgment" – as in, this is the reason God will judge the world – "The light has come into the world and people loved the darkness rather than the light because their works were evil. For everyone who does wicked things hates the light and does not come to the light, lest his works should be exposed." (John 3:19-20)

When you try to live out loud what God has done for you, there are many who will hate you. They will try to extinguish the light that you shine. Don't be surprised when the opposition comes. But remember the good news:

> "The light shines in the darkness, and the darkness has not overcome it." (John 1:5)

Don't let Satan *poof* it out. Let it shine.

ONE STEP IN THE RIGHT DIRECTION

You've gone into the wilderness, you've met God, you've passed through the waters and now you've returned. You are the agent of change that God has commissioned. This might be daunting. Very often we'd rather ourselves be changed, but leave our family out of it, or our business. But this is what you were born for. It's time to start living out the life that God has assigned to you.

It's time to start thinking about practical steps you can take to bring the light of God into your world. Some of these will be obvious, like addressing the situation that catapulted you into the wilderness in the first place. Others will be more subtle, like attitude problems, or festering relationships. And some will be exceedingly difficult, like disentangling yourself from a life of deception or even criminality in which you find yourself stuck.

This begins by taking responsibility for the world around you, including the people who live in it. You've got to be prudent with this one, because you cannot live life for somebody else, and many things are out of your control. But you can choose to be responsible for bringing encouraging words to a difficult person, or doing more than your share to maintain your marriage. And while you may feel powerless in your state or your city, you can at least commit to not making it worse. Sometimes even those little things have an astonishing ripple effect.

Look at how John the Baptist addressed those who came to him.

"The crowds asked him, 'What then shall we do?' And he answered them, Whoever has two tunics is to share with him who has none, and whoever has food is to do likewise.'" (Luke 3:10-11)

233

This is an example of general principles. If you don't know how to begin living your new life, you can start with general things.

Start with some of the great biblical "don'ts". Don't steal. Work hard for what you get and pay for it fairly. This seems so basic, but if a community cannot trust the honesty of its commerce, it goes downhill very quickly. Don't kill. Jesus would add to that not to hate anybody. Don't indulge in violent behavior, but learn to control yourself and handle problems peacefully. Don't lie, and live your life in such a way that you don't have to.

You could move on to the great "do's". Love your neighbor as yourself. That just about covers everything, doesn't it? Treat other people the way you want to be treated, consider their needs first and then meet those needs. Honor your father and your mother. Better yet, maintain the integrity and love of the whole family. Don't let it fall apart on your watch. You be the one to make the tough phone calls and broker peace. Rejoice always, the Bible says. Determine to take a joyful position in life, and it will be contagious. If God has changed your life and forgiven your sins, is that not a good enough reason to be happy?

There are all manner of general principles that we should be following. Search the Scriptures and learn them well. Follow the example of godly people, and you will see the results. God doesn't tell us to do things just because He's bossy. He knows what is best, and He has been proven right time and again.

There were others who came to John the Baptist.

"Tax collectors also came to be baptized and said to him, 'Teacher, what shall we do?' And he said to them, 'Collect no more than you are authorized to do.' Soldiers also asked him, 'And we, what shall we do?' And he said to them, 'Do not extort money from anyone by threats or by false accusation, and be content with your wages.'" (Luke 3:12-14)

We are all to obey general commandments, but God has a specific word for each one of our lives. You must find out what yours is.

Too many Christians hide behind general principles in order to avoid the very specific thing we ought to do. We go to church, we tithe, we watch our language, we don't indulge in sexual sin – but we refuse to call our brother and forgive him. It is this kind of cop-out that God did not allow Jacob, and will not allow you.

So what is your specific commandment? Do you need to move out of your girlfriend's house and stop committing fornication? Do you need to quit your job because it forces you to harass downtrodden people? Do you need to tell your sister that her aggression toward your children will not be tolerated anymore? Do you need to stop spending every dollar you make, in order to secure a future for yourself? Do you need to erase your drug dealer's phone number and change your own? Do you need to start presenting as your God-given gender? Do you need to tell your husband you love him without expecting anything in return? Do you need to delete your Instagram account?

I can't tell you exactly what you need to do. Only God can do that. Believe me, He will not hide it from you. But once you know, you've got to do it. Don't let the size of what you've been called to do intimidate you from stepping out. God doesn't need you to fix your whole life in one day. He just needs you to take one real step in the right direction. The best part is that when you do, you will find that you are up to the challenge. God is with you. By your courage, you just might set off a chain of divine dominoes.

HEROES AND HERALDS

The Bible mostly narrates the highlights of its heroes' lives. That's good storytelling. But we mustn't forget that after these men and women had their life-changing encounters with God, they became change agents that built up the lives of the people around them. Let them serve as your inspiration, for they are your brothers indeed.

We have several great stories about Daniel. He was taken from his home and exiled to Babylon, where he refused to partake of the king's delicacies. He interpreted dreams of the kings and was eventually thrown into the lion's den for his faithfulness. But the second half of the book of Daniel narrates what came after. Daniel was instrumental in helping the children of Israel return from Exile, both through his prayers and his influence at the Persian court. Not only that, but God gave him some of the most amazing prophecies of things that had not yet come to pass. Through them we learn that God is in control of history, and that it will all end with a smashing triumph from Jesus Christ. Daniel's story did not end after his big miracle, most of his best work was just getting started.

We've talked an awful lot about Peter in this book. I think many of us feel a kindred spirit with the hasty apostle. But after his moment of restoration with Christ, Peter would go on to lead the early Church. He preached the first Gospel message and performed one of the first high-profile miracles. He was beaten and arrested, and was forced to travel around, where he did even more mighty works. It was Peter who brought the Gentiles into the Church for the first time. It was Peter who penned two of the books of our New Testament, and probably inspired the Gospel of Mark. He would eventually die on a cross upside-down, claiming he was not worthy to die the same way as his Lord. There was so much more to his life than his tragicomic banter with Jesus. He was an agent of leadership and transformation.

Elijah required a rebuke from the Lord to get back into gear after his big moment. Following his years in the wilderness, he called down fire from heaven on Mount Carmel, leading the execution of the false priests, and praying back life-giving rain to the land. But Queen Jezebel sent assassins to destroy him, and he fled back to the wilderness. He asked for God to take his life because he was so despondent that nothing had really changed. God told him to buck up and get back, because He was not finished telling his story. Elijah had a long ministry after this, known as "the chariots of Israel and its horsemen" (2 Kings 2:12). Most of this is unrecorded, except for his discipleship of the prophet Elisha, who would exceed even his accomplishments. Elijah had a great story, but there was much more to come afterward.

I could go on. Joseph's story was not complete until he had made provision for his family in the land of Egypt. Moses needed to shepherd his people in the wilderness, and write down the record of God's Law. Elisha had to return across the river and take up Elijah's mantle, David sat on the throne for forty years. Just because you have had your big moment does not mean your story is over. It means you are now ready to begin your story. You can step into your calling and live it out, quietly and maybe even thanklessly.

Don't let yourself get discouraged like Elijah if your whole world doesn't fall into place at the first epiphany. Problems that took a lifetime to make will take a long time to resolve. The labor is largely done in obscurity, and most people are not going to appreciate it, especially at first. Emily Dickinson wrote over 1,800 poems, only publishing ten during her lifetime. It was only upon her death that her friends and family realized what a genius she was. Life is long, and it takes work. But in Christ you are equal to the task. And the world needs you to step up.

In the War of 1812, the *USS Chesapeake* was in a fierce battle against the Royal Navy. A young third lieutenant named William Sitgreaves Cox commanded a gun crew belowdecks. As the battle raged, all his men were killed or scattered. He went up top and saw the captain mortally wounded. Quickly, he grabbed his captain and took him to the surgeon. Was he rewarded for his bravery? William Sitgreaves Cox was court-martialed and convicted for abandoning his post. It turned out that every officer above him had been incapacitated. He was in command of the ship when he took the captain to the infirmary. He was the next man up, and because he did not know it, the ship was leaderless and lost.

You may think that you will never be the next man up, there are far too many above you. But you can't think that way. You've got to take responsibility for the life you've been given, and grab hold of that helm with confidence. Everyone else is depending on you.

LOVE THEM ENOUGH

Jacob was broken, and had broken his family. In the wilderness, God transformed him, and he became an agent of transformation. You are not all that God has called you to be, but He does not hold that against you. He is ready to turn you around and send you back to shine your light into the darkness.

But it can be cold and lonely when you look around and realize that the cavalry isn't coming. It's just you. I want to acknowledge that fear, and I don't want to minimize it. But I must remind you of why we live this way. It cannot just be for ourselves, because then we won't do any of it. Maybe you've read through this book only thinking about yourself and your personal growth or improvement. If that is the case, I want to add to you the one crucial ingredient – love.

"Beloved, let us love one another, for love is from God, and whoever loves has been born of God and knows God. Anyone who does not love does not know God, because God is love. In this the love of God was made manifest among us, that God sent his only Son into the world, so that we might live through him." (1 John 4:7-9)

John wrote that. He called us beloved, and we are. We are loved by God. We only know love because of God. And if you have a heart full of love, then you truly know God. But if you harden your heart to love, then you do not know God. The Apostle goes as far as to say that, "God is love". And then he gives us the Gospel. God showed his love to us by sending His Son to die on the cross for the forgiveness of our sins. God's love is an active, participatory, incarnational love. "So that we might live through him." That's the next step. We are to do as Christ did by demonstrating love to one another.

That's a motivation that will last much longer than the latest *ra-ra* inspirational song. When you are not just living out your calling for yourself, but for your family, or your countrymen, then you can find the strength to keep going. Perhaps you need to pray and ask God to give you a love for the people around you. He'll answer that prayer. He wants to share His heart with you so that you can share His heart with the world.

Love is willing to sacrifice itself. That's what all this has been about; becoming the kind of person whose life can be used to make everything else right. We are the vessels of God; we are tools in His

239

hand. That is why this cannot just be you living your dreams. You don't know what you need, and you don't know what the world needs. God does. That is why He constrains the possibilities of our lives, out of love. Love for you and love for those whom you will love in turn.

So love them, my brother. Love them enough to spend your own life for their sake. The cavalry is not coming. You are the cavalry. Ride for yourself, and you'll fall in the battle. Ride out of obligation, and you'll run away. Ride out of love for those you have ridden to save, and you will change the world.

STUDY QUESTIONS

1.) Do you remember the first time you were the adult in the room? How must an adult think differently about their life?

2.) Is it hard to grasp that your mundane acts of obedience can make a huge difference? Why is it easier to focus on the "big issues" than our own lives?

3.) If Jacob had not humbled himself, how might Esau have greeted him differently? Have you ever had a reconciliation with a family member? Does that affect how you read stories like this one?

4.) How was this episode of his life a turning point for Jacob? Are you approaching a turning point like this one?

5.) What does it mean to be salt and light? Have you been living up to that calling? How could you start today?

6.) Has anyone ever tried to extinguish your light? Have you ever struggled to keep it shining because of your own insecurities?

7.) What are some general principles from the Bible that you could start following right away? How might your life improve if you did them wholeheartedly?

8.) What is one specific thing that you should be doing to obey God? Why have you not done this yet? When are you going to do it? How will your life get better? How will it get worse if you don't?

9.) Where are you the "next man up" in your life? Is it time that you took command in the fight against sin?

10.) Why is love a better motivation than ambition or guilt? What is your motivation for spiritual transformation? Ask Jesus to give you love for those whom you will serve.

CONCLUSION

MASTERS OF THE WILDERNESS

DESERT POWER

One of the most epic stories of the Bible is that of Absalom's rebellion. It has everything you need for a good story: battle, betrayal, spies, intrigue and a tragic ending that will break your heart. In it, David's son Absalom rebelled against him and drove him from Jerusalem, across the Jordan to Mahanaim (where Jacob had wrestled with God). Ahithophel, Absalom's counselor at court, advised him to ride out with twelve thousand men and slay the king. But Hushai, David's mole in the palace, gave different advice. He said,

> "You know that your father and his men are mighty men, and that they are enraged, like a bear robbed of her cubs in the field. Besides, your father is an expert in war; he will not spend the night with the

people. Behold, even now he has hidden himself in one of the pits or in some other place." (2 Samuel 17:8-9)

He gave further advice, but it is this description of David that I want to focus on here at the end.

Hushai warned Absalom against trying to fight his father in the wilderness. He reminded him that David was "a mighty [man]...enraged, like a bear robbed of her cubs". He called him "an expert in war," reminding him of the years when David eluded Saul in the wild without capture. The would-be king was reminded that his father had been in the wilderness before. He was comfortable there, he was strong there, and Absalom had made a terrible mistake by driving David out of the city. David was a master of the wilderness, and that made him unstoppable, even against impossible odds.

It's like the words of Japanese Admiral Yamamoto after the destruction of Pearl Harbor: "I fear all we have done is to awaken a sleeping giant and fill him with a terrible resolve," he warned. He knew that America was a mighty, industrial power, and Japan had just forced themselves into a war of attrition against her. The battle was now to be fought where their enemy was strong.

In the book, *Dune*, the Grand Duke Leto Atreides is given the right to rule over the desert planet Arrakis. He knows that in order to control the economic gem, he will need to cultivate a different kind of strength than what he is used to. "Desert Power" he calls it. To gain such power, he must look to the native Fremen, who have lived among the dunes for generations and mastered its ways.

David had Desert Power. It was his home, his natural habitat. He was hardened there into a man who could rule Israel well. So when Absalom rebelled, and he was forced to flee into the wilderness, he was ready. In fact, he had just been handed a great advantage. Because he had faced the wilderness before, he was not afraid to be driven there again. The moment he entered the wilderness, the odds shifted in his favor.

John the Baptist had Desert Power. "He was in the wilderness" (Luke 1:80), eating locusts and honey, learning the voice of the Lord and disciplining his body to obey, until the day God sent him to the Jordan. What could you do to threaten a man like that? What hardship could possibly deter him, what luxury could possibly tempt him? John was a master of the wilderness, not just physically, but spiritually as well.

Athanasius was the bishop of Alexandria in Egypt. During the Arian crisis, the Roman empire tried to enforce heretical doctrines upon the Church. Athanasius was, for a time, the only prominent voice to take a hard public stand against the Arian emperors. They called him *Athanasius Contra Mundum*, meaning "Athanasius Against the World". During his life, he was banished five times.

One such occasion took place on February 8, 356 A.D. Emperor Constantius sent five thousand soldiers to surround the Church of St. Theonas, where he knew Athanasius was preaching. The congregation barred the doors while Athanasius set them to singing Psalm 136, with its mighty refrain, "For his steadfast love endures forever". The other leaders urged him to run, but he refused to leave until he could be sure that the people would be safe. As the soldiers burst through the doors, his flock rushed to hold them back so their shepherd could get away.

Athanasius fled to the desert. Letting him get away was a foolish error on Rome's part. Athanasius had spent time among the monks, discipled by Anthony the Great himself. So when he arrived at their cells, they spirited him away and hid him for years. Athanasius was a

245

master of the wilderness, and he had some serious Desert Power. During his exile, he wrote books that would resolve the theological controversies and bring the true Church back together. He would outlast every heretic and pagan emperor who opposed him and see the faith restored to its original purity.

And of course the ultimate master of the wilderness was Jesus Christ. After His baptism, He spent forty days there fasting and facing the temptations of Satan. During His ministry, He would often "withdraw to desolate places and pray" (Luke 5:16). Jesus made a habit of entering the wilderness to be strengthened for His work. To put Jesus in a corner, to force Him to navigate uncomfortable, hostile situations, was to put Him right where He wanted to be.

How many others could we list? Moses, Elijah, Paul – all masters of the wilderness, full of God-given Desert Power.

If you have followed this book to the end, then you have had your own sojourn in the spiritual wilderness. You have seen the end of yourself and repented of that sin. You have been broken in God's hands and passed through the waters to return to the Promised Land. You have gained a little Desert Power of your own!

I urge you to master the wilderness. Make it your home, your frequent abode. Take this journey not just once, but often. Use the life of Jacob as your example to conquer bad habits and besetting sins, bad breaks and broken hearts. Like Jesus, go repeatedly into the wilderness to commune with your Father and return home a little better each time.

Then when the world rocks beneath your feet, when Satan buffets you with temptations and tribulations, and you are driven into the wilderness of necessity? You will be ready. You will be a sleeping giant, ready to face the trials coming your way. You will have traversed these sands before, and you will know exactly what to do. Others will look to you in those moments, and you will no longer be a fugitive, but a guide. You'll have Holy Spirit Desert Power that will make the Devil rue the day he ever thought he could mess with you.

THE MOST IMPORTANT THING

I hope this book has been a helpful roadmap for you as you've made your way to the wilderness and back. But there is one journey that we all must take, and if you have read this book without understanding the need for it, then I will have failed miserably.

You have a destiny that God has prepared for you. He desires for you to live forever with Him in the new world that He is going to create at the end of days. Not only that, He desires you to have abundance in the life you're living right now. He's a good father who only wants the best for His children.

But you are dead in your sins. You are corrupted by the cancer that has infected the whole world, and God must judge it with eternity in Hell. There is no escaping this, no matter how pleasant your life may seem.

You've got to shake yourself awake. You've got to be disrupted in the normal day-to-day of your life. This way of living is not good, and it's going to end in the loss of your soul. You are not promised tomorrow. You cannot wait, you must act now.

So out into the wilderness with you! Prepare yourself to be changed! Can we at least agree that Hell would be a bad thing? That you are not perfect, and that God cannot tolerate imperfection? Then step out into the desert with me so that you can hear His voice.

For God will speak to you. He is speaking to you right now. His Holy Spirit is drawing you to Himself. He is convicting you of sin and assuring you of the coming judgment. But if you will trust Him, He will guide you through this desert and bring you back better than before. There is hope, if you will follow His lead.

Let Him show you that monster in the mirror. You are not okay just as you are. And you are not just in need of a few tweaks, you are irreparably damaged. If you allow yourself to continue down the road of sin, you are going to end up miserable and broken and dead.

You might think you can handle it. You might think you can manage your vices, but I assure you that you are wrong. I hope you don't have to struggle for long, but if you need to test this truth, do it quickly. When you fight against yourself, you will always lose.

So are you ready to renounce that old life? Are you ready to turn around and walk the other way? You must repent and change your mind, agree with God's evaluation of you. His is the only one that matters after all. Turn to Him and ask, "What must I do?"

Only then will He lead you back. This is no otherworldly, ethereal experience. God wants to send you back to the life that you have been ruining. This is real-world stuff, you are going to have to face the very thing that frightens you most. What is the one thing you would never give up or change about yourself? That is the price of admission.

For it is time to die my friend. It is time to accept the death of Jesus Christ for the forgiveness of your sins. You deserve death, but Jesus took it for you on the cross. And He rose again on the third day as evidence that everything He said is true, and that His sacrifice has been accepted by God. You must die to yourself and choose to place your hope only in the risen Christ Jesus. Everything goes on the altar, everything burns up. Believe and confess that Jesus is Lord, and you will be saved. Refuse, and you await a wretched eternity of torment and death, to say nothing of a life of fruitless wandering in the dry, lonely wilderness.

But if you repent and believe, then you will be born again! God will give you a new name that redeems all the best parts of your identity. He will wipe away all the guilt that is against you and write your name in His Book of Life. The past will be gone, and only a glorious future will remain.

Then it's time to shine your light. Go out to the world and let them know the joy and hope and peace and love that you have found. Let the love of God that saved you spread to everyone you meet. Make things right, work to bring about good changes, be the cavalry that everyone is waiting for.

"For God so loved the world, that he gave his only Son, that whoever believes in him should not perish but have eternal life." (John 3:16)

That's the Good News. Once you have walked that road into the wilderness, you will always be at home there. Any other journey will seem light by comparison.

STRUGGLE AND SURRENDER

The life of Jacob is so real and so raw that it always motivates me to move forward. If God could take a man like that and turn him into the patriarch of His chosen people, then there must be hope for folks like you and me. This is such a better story than the sickly-sweet platitudes about everyone being special. And it's certainly a more hopeful one than the despair over existence that so many feel compelled to accept. Your life is part of God's cosmic plan to save the whole world. So live it out! Embrace the struggle, the struggle is real.

Struggle & Surrender

God is not afraid to wrestle with you. But remember that the key to victory is surrender.

Whoever you are, know that I love you and God does too. Let's walk this road together, with Christ as our guide and our companion. Because that's how we save the world – one life and one step at a time.

STUDY QUESTIONS

1.) Why was David strong in the wilderness? How does this apply to our understanding of the spiritual wilderness?

2.) Why is it important to be strong in the spirit before the crisis comes? How could a strong, spiritual guide have helped you during your sojourn in the wilderness?

3.) Which sections of this book spoke to you the most? What actions do you need to take going forward?

4.) Have you believed on the Lord Jesus Christ? Have you been forgiven of your sins and saved from death and Hell? Why or why not? It's time to take that plunge, God is waiting for you.

5.) What does it mean to "struggle and surrender"? Are you glad for the struggle? Have you fully surrendered?

THE END

THANKS FOR READING!

For more resources from Pastor Tyler Warner, including free eBooks, recorded Bible teachings, and devotional videos, you can visit **CalvaryChapelTrussville.com**.

To connect with Calvary Chapel Trussville, you can check Facebook, Instagram and YouTube for regular content.

And if you were blessed by this book, please get in touch with us and let us know. We'd be delighted to know you!

Calvary Chapel Trussville

5239 Old Springville Rd, Pinson, AL, 35126
CalvaryChapelTrussville.com
Office@CalvaryChapelTrussville.com

ALSO BY PASTOR TYLER:

Available in print, eBook and audiobook on
Amazon or **CalvaryChapelTrussville.com**

Made in USA - Kendallville, IN
63148_9780578330761
01.19.2022 0920